Praise for

WEALTH

Through Real Estate Investing

"Real Estate investing—we have all contemplated it but have been dissuaded by lack of knowledge. Finally, here is a book that sets out comprehensively and practically—based on the author's extensive personal experience—the benefits and pitfalls of investing in Real Estate." —David Jebb, LLB, BSc.—Real Estate Lawyer.

"*The Brij Team* has become one of the top performing teams in North America, achieving *The elite Circle of Legends*, *Hall of Fame* and the *Luminary of Distinction* awards—the highest awards a Realtor can receive within the RE/MAX organization. Jay is one of the most prolific performers in its 40-year history. *Wealth Through Real Estate Investing* is easy to read, understand and implement. I really like the way Jay puts theory into practice. —Frank Colatosti, CEO, RE/MAX West Realty Inc.

"Jay is one of the top professionals in the Real Estate realm. With over 30 years experience, he's navigated through every economic high and low, coming out winning every time. Jay's accumulated wisdom will give you the knowledge you need to achieve success." —Grant Browning, President/ CEO, *Toronto Caribbean News Inc.*

"Jay Brijpaul has tapped his vast experience and expertise in the Real Estate industry and written *Wealth, Through Real Estate Investing.*" —Ken Puddicombe, CPA (retired Controller, Finance), author of *Racing With The Rain, Junta and Down Independence Boulevard and Other Stories.*

"Real estate investment can seem complex for many individuals, but this book provides a simple step by step approach on what's needed to understand and navigate its constant changing world." —G. Chatwal, CPA, CA

MiddleRoad|Publishers

27/APR/24
To BRIAN
This is your
map to

WEALTH

Through Real Estate Investing

By

Jay Brijpaul, BSc, FRI

MiddleRoad | Publishers

www.middleroadpublishers.ca

Making Literature See The Light Of Day

Library and Archives Canada Cataloguing in Publication

Brijpaul, Jay, Author

Wealth Through Real Estate Investing

ISBN 978-1-9991365-4-3 (softcover)

Editor: Ken Puddicombe www.kenpud.wordpress.com

Cover Design by Adit Creative Marketing Programming

www.adit.com

WEALTH

Through Real Estate Investing

"*Real estate is an imperishable asset, ever increasing in value. It is the most solid security that human ingenuity has devised. It is the basis of all security and about the only indestructible security.*"
—Russell Sage (August 4, 1816 – July 22, 1906), financier, railroad executive and Whig politician from New York, United States.

DEDICATION

To my loving wife Nan without whose support I
could not have reached where I am today, and to our
four children, Akash, Anjie, Videsh and Kavita for their
confidence in me.

WEALTH

Through Real Estate Investing

EDITOR'S NOTE

While this book offers valuable insight into the Real Estate industry, it is not meant to be *the* solution for achieving wealth.

Jay Brijpaul has laid out his approach in simple, easy-to-follow steps, based on his cumulative thirty years-knowledge of the Real Estate in Canada. With this knowledge has come experience that has allowed him to excel and be one of the top practitioners in his field.

The principles espoused by the author, apart from the tax implications which differ from jurisdiction to jurisdiction, hold true for any free-market real-estate environment. While readers will find valuable tips for achieving financial independence and security through real estate investment, the author and publisher accept no responsibility and will not be held liable for investments that don't meet readers' expectations.

Ken Puddicombe, CPA, CMA   Jay Brijpaul BSc, FRI

Editor   Author

www.middleroadpublishers.ca

ACKNOWLEDGMENTS

The information in this book is taken from lectures given and columns published by me in various publications over many years, including *Indo Caribbean World* and *Toronto Caribbean Newspaper*.

Thanks to my daughter Anjie and my son Akash who assisted me to bring this book to fruition. Nan, my life and my wife, thanks for all you have done; from your subtle suggestions to your loving touch, I am blessed. To my younger two children, Videsh and Kavita, thanks for guidance and suggestions.

To my editor, Ken Puddicombe. Thanks for telling me that I can do it. Your insights, patience and encouragement are invaluable.

Table of Contents

SECTION 1: INTRODUCTION

1.01 FOREWORD

My purpose in writing this book is to help you light the path towards your financial freedom.

My road towards successful real estate investing has not been straightforward and on the way, I learned that those who venture out by themselves to learn-by-doing risk getting lost along the way—much like I did over thirty years ago. The learning curve is steep, and the lack of preparation can be costly. On the other hand, the upside is tremendous. I hope that this book will not only spark your interest in real estate but allow you to see more clearly how to prepare for this remarkable journey and the pitfalls to avoid.

You might be wondering what makes this book special. It is a distillation of my decades of experience as both a real estate agent and an investor. Having attained financial freedom through real estate, over the years I have learned what works and what is best avoided. So, I didn't need to write a book to capitalize further on real-estate investing, and my sole purpose is to pass on my expertise to you. (The proceeds from the sale of this book are strictly for charity.)

This book is my contribution to a career and a lifestyle that allowed me to provide for my family, arriving in Canada as an immigrant with no savings to rely on. It starts from my first steps in building wealth, in the early spring of life, to disposing of assets and starting to wind down in the late grey autumn days.

It is my desire that the reader will be prepared for the challenges ahead, armed with the practical knowledge necessary to embark on this journey towards financial freedom.

THE BEST INVESTMENT ON EARTH

My Journey to Financial Freedom: Learning Lessons the Hard Way

When I first came to Canada, I knew nothing about real estate. My first residence was an apartment in Scarborough, Lyn Valley. I was advised by friends and relatives to buy the best furniture and appliances because when I eventually bought my home, I could keep them. That was my very first mistake. Consider that back then in 1987, one-bedroom condos were selling for about $40,000. All I needed was $4,000 down. However, based on the advice I had received, I decided instead to buy an expensive bedroom set for the same price. Since my goal was to build wealth, I had already made my first mistake in real estate. The lesson? Be careful whose advice you follow. You should not go to the mechanic when your head hurts or to the doctor when your car breaks down. Consider the experience attached to the opinion.

When I bought my first home, I relied on a friend who introduced me to a realtor. The realtor showed me a home in Malton and convinced me to buy it. The sellers were his friends and they eventually bought another home from him. The home I bought was roach-infested and required work. Unknown to me at the time, I also paid above market value. The realtor assisted me in arranging a mortgage through a broker. This resulted in exorbitant brokerage fees as well as a first and second mortgage. The lesson? Get another, independent opinion. These days, I interview at least three people before deciding. This costly mistake was another detour on my journey to financial freedom.

Over the decades that I have practiced real estate and invested, I assisted many people financially and received the short end of the stick. I once assisted a client who relocated to Mexico with an outstanding loan. She asked if I could help, promising to repay in a few weeks. It has been over 10 years now, and I am still hoping to see the money. The lesson? If someone does not have the money in the first place, there is good reason to suspect you will not be repaid. If you must lend money to such a person, it is best to simply give and forget rather than to lend and repent.

In the mid 90's, my friend, a top-notch accountant, advised me to have a mixed investment portfolio. I had a few rental properties then and with his advice, I bought mutual funds. About seven years later, I sold these at a loss and moved on. I had no expertise in such funds and only succeeded in paying the managers (management fees) and advisors (trailer fees) who made money while my investments stagnated. The lesson here? I learned to stick to what I know best. Had I stuck to my area of expertise and used the money to buy a few more rental properties, I would have been on an express flight to financial freedom.

Oscar Wilde, the famous poet and playwright, once said "Experience is simply the name we give our mistakes." Throughout my decades of experience as a realtor and investor, I have learned the hard way from thousands and thousands of similar lessons, through countless mistakes. The purpose of this book is to distil my decades of experience into practical wisdom to assist you on your path to financial freedom. By studying the contents of this book, you will be able to learn from my experience while avoiding many of the mistakes I made along the way.

1.02 WHY REAL ESTATE?

Imagine an investment which is always in demand. Land is a finite resource. As populations grow exponentially, the demand for real estate follows. As a result, it acts as a hedge against inflation. Put simply, if prospective homeowners have more money, they will pay more to outbid other potential buyers. Inflation also benefits the real estate investor since today's dollar is worth more than tomorrow's dollar (eroded due to inflation). Your ability to pay off the mortgage increases as the mortgage loan dilutes over the years from inflation, while your income hopefully grows to match it.

A great tradesman requires the right tools for the job and must understand how to use them. Similarly in real estate, there are some fundamental building blocks which you must understand before assembling your "real estate toolkit."

THE LEVER PRINCIPLE

A lever is an instrument that is used to lift heavy loads with the least amount of effort. The longer the lever, the greater the lifting power. The lever, or "leverage", allows you to own large investments with a minimum down payment. Your assets represent your lever—the more assets you have, the larger your real estate lever.

Let's assume that you purchase a property for $600,000 and you invest 10% of your own money. Your initial investment is therefore $60,000. If the property increases by 10% in one year, then it is worth $660,000.

In this example, your initial investment doubles! You invested $60,000 and made $60,000. That's an impressive 100% growth. A buyer may invest 10% of his own money and own 100% of the property. The other 90% is loaned to you.

However, there are risks. In a declining housing market, it can be detrimental. If the value of the property drops by 10% in the above example, the down payment evaporates. With multiple properties the loss can be substantial. My advice is to gauge your risk tolerance and do not spread yourself financially thin.

CONCENTRIC CIRCLES

Imagine a pool of water. If you throw a pebble into the center of a swimming pool, the first ripple it makes is the largest. Subsequent ripples become smaller until they level off toward the end.

Let's look at a city the same way. The circle at the center represents the downtown core and the circle toward the end represents the surrounding suburbs. Like the rippling effect, there is more activity in the downtown core because of jobs and transportation. For this reason, homes downtown are more expensive than those in the suburbs. In a strong market, homes in the center appreciate faster and, in a recession, homes in the outer circle depreciate faster. The "concentric circle" principle also applies to a smaller area where an economic hub represents the center.

Always look at the center of action and buy close to it. There are times where the economic center may shift, for example, a new state of the art shopping center will be the new center of action and the concentric circle could shift.

PROGRESSION AND REGRESSION

The principle of progression states that in an upscale neighborhood, the smallest home on the block will increase substantially in value because of the surrounding area. The principle of regression is when the value of the biggest home on the block decreases because of the smaller homes in the surrounding area.

Buying a home is like a three-level cake. The base represents the location and is the most valuable part of the cake. The middle represents the size of the property, and the top represents any upgrades. Upgrades are in fact like icing on the cake. One can always upgrade a larger home but cannot always expand a smaller home

Using the principle of progression and regression, it is better to buy the cheapest home in the most upscale locality than to buy the most expensive home in a less well-off area.

SUBSTITUTION

David Knox, a world-renowned real estate speaker and author, explains this principle using two homes, side by side, each with a well.

The first owner spent $20,000 to install the well but the next-door neighbor had to dig deeper and his well cost $30,000. Their costs are different, but the value of the homes is the same because both homes have water.

Value is a function of what you get out of a property and not what you put into it. An owner can easily spend thousands of dollars to modernize but if the size has not changed and the function remains the same then the value will not change substantially.

Most owners upgrade a home because of enjoyment and not the resale value. Here is another way of looking at it; assuming an owner's renovation budget is $50,000, he can use the money to modernize the home or to make a basement apartment. He will get some pleasure from the modernization but by making a basement apartment, the function of the property changes and so the value will increase.

THE WATERFALLS

Think of real estate demand as a waterfall. When prices are high in one area, the overflow will travel towards the next lower priced area. For example, prices in Mississauga, Ontario are higher than Brampton, Ontario and any spillover may "flow" into Brampton, impacting prices.

It is best to invest in good residential homes in a city which will benefit from spillover in the long term, but where the prices are currently cheaper. By doing so, you allow more room for growth.

Most people do not plan to fail but they simply fail to plan. Like a good farmer, use the tools above to decide where to till the soil and plant the seeds. With time, your investment will blossom.

WHAT TO BUY

Freehold properties make good investments. It is smart to buy homes on large lots in mature sections of town. The growth potential is higher for the longer term. As the city expands, developers will buy these homes and tear down and rebuild larger homes. Once this happens, the value of your property will climb drastically (the principle of progression).

Bread and butter properties—the ones that are simple and affordable, are the easiest to rent. The idea: multiple smaller, more affordable homes are better investments than one large home. I knew of a few investors who invested in million-dollar homes. The problem they all ran into was that the rent was not adequate to service both the mortgage and property tax while keeping cash flow positive. Smaller homes are easier to rent and cheaper to maintain. Also, in the event of an emergency or the need for liquidity, they are easier to sell. If you buy freehold, consider buying homes away from apartment buildings since you risk diminishing your chance to attract model long-term tenants. Your property value can plummet overnight if there is even one major incident with drugs and other crime in the area.

SPECULATING OR INVESTING?

An investment must always match the investor's appetite for risk. This raises an often-asked question: "How risky is investing in real estate?" The answer lies in the difference between an investor and a speculator.

The speculator's goal is to make a quick profit. Examples include flipping houses or paying a condominium deposit with the goal of having the interest later assigned for a higher price. Acting as a speculator requires a high-risk tolerance. In the late 80's, asking prices in the housing market climbed at an alarming rate. Speculators, intent on flipping homes, purchased properties closing, on average, within two years. Despite an enduring long-term demand for housing, the market temporarily crashed in the 90's. Many speculators lost everything, including their own homes.

The investor reduces his or her risk by focusing on the long-term, thereby maximizing both security and profit. Risk is assessed one good deal at a time, buying opportunistically when others are selling.

My advice? Avoid speculating and focus on investing. As you learn and internalize the rules of this book, consider increasing your risk tolerance upon consulting a licensed professional.

PITFALLS ALONG THE ROAD

The word "mistake" carries the connotation that we "missed the take!" While I believe all mistakes are learning opportunities, there are some common pitfalls to avoid.

1. NOT EXPLAINING YOUR GOALS TO YOUR REALTOR. Everyone has different goals, and a good realtor can adapt to what you need provided they understand your circumstances and situation. An experienced realtor can save you thousands by, e.g., advising you to get an open mortgage if your goal is to flip a property.

2. BUYING A HOME WITHOUT HAVING AN INSPECTION. A professional inspection may allow you to renegotiate with the seller. Remember, knowledge is power! In situations where there are multiple offers, buyers may want to inspect the home before the offer date. An experienced investor

knows the tricks of the trade and can negotiate accordingly.

3. HAVING AN ESCAPE CLAUSE or a condition for financing will give you, the prospective investor, time to consider and, if necessary, rethink the offer. Experienced investors would remove conditions and offer a lower buying price to the seller. In this case, removing the conditions becomes a bargaining tool.

4. BUYING OUT-OF-THE-AREA PROPERTY WITHOUT PROPER RESEARCH. Sometimes our emotions can blindside us from potential dangers associated with out-of-town purchases.

COSTS TO CONSIDER

Real estate typically requires significant capital upfront. For example, bank sales and distress sale properties are often sold "as is" and require repairs. For this reason, it is important to work through the math from start to finish, making sure the investment is viable. Seasoned investors can sometimes see danger lurking beneath the camouflage or a diamond waiting to be found and polished.

If you are buying, renovating, and flipping a property, you should factor in the following costs for purchasing:

- Land transfer tax (in some jurisdictions)
- Lawyer's fees

- CMHC fees (in Ontario) for high ratio mortgages (homes purchased with less than 20% down payment at time of writing)
- Disbursements

Upon purchase and closing, the investor must then carry the following costs, typically for about three months, while the home is being repaired or renovated and then sold:

- Property tax
- Mortgage payments
- Utilities
- Materials and contractor cost
- Real Estate fees (upon sale only)
- Lawyer fees for closing (upon sale only)

An average home will take two months to close, impacting your bottom line. In addition, these homes are unlikely to sell significantly above market value. As an investor, you must be realistic about your asking price. Consider further that a buyer purchasing a property above market price may be turned down for financing by his or her lender if the appraisal value suggests a lower valuation.

In addition to these factors, when flipping a property, you should consider the following:

- Property location. What makes the location "hot"?

- Hard costs for renovating. For example, materials and mortgage payments will remain the same but a property's location will have a major impact on the selling price

- Tax implications. Absent the "principal residence exemption," the sale of a house will be a taxable event

Rather than selling a home and paying all the hard costs and sales tax, it is better to:

1. Renovate it, so that the value would increase.
2. Increase the mortgage and scoop the equity.
3. Rent the newly renovated home at a premium.

I worked with a few investors who bought, renovated, and flipped homes. I advised them to rent, but they were more focused on liquid cash. Today, with inflation, home prices have sky-rocketed, and their liquid cash is watered down.

KNOW YOUR ABCs—ALWAYS BE CAREFUL

In real estate people can be taken advantage of if they're not familiar with the process. For example, one family I knew refinanced their home and the mortgage broker they used got a private first, second and third mortgage. The lender fees, mortgage broker fees and lawyer fees were outrageous. The owners had originally bought their home for $550,000 with $200,000 as a down payment. The home recently sold for $900,000 but the three mortgages on the property added up to be $1,100,000. The third mortgage was a blanket mortgage, registered on their parents' home as well. The shortfall on closing remained as a high interest mortgage on their parents' property.

Real estate involves various aspects—from financing to foreclosure. For many, most of their wealth is in their home. Be wary of others sizing up your property.

DEVELOPING A WINNING TEAM

The best place to start is by educating yourself. Avoid using investment clubs and experts who promise to make you a millionaire overnight. Investing is like gardening. Choose a sunny spot (good location), prepare the soil (do your homework), plant the seeds (don't delay), water the plants (take care of your investment) and in time, it will blossom.

Equip yourself with a good realtor, inspector, lawyer, mortgage broker, accountant and a few trades people or contractors. It is also important to seek out professionals who have investment properties. People with experience are potential mentors and can guide you. Once you find the right fit, work with your professionals, and learn from the experts. If they find you are loyal, they will go out of their way to help you.

LESSONS LEARNED

- Always seek professional advice

- Share your objectives in buying, investing, or speculating with your realtor

- Set conditions, including an "escape clause" and a "condition for financing", into your offer

- Consider ALL costs involved in the purchase

- Do a cost/benefit analysis on the property

- Avoid making snap decisions

1.03 ART OF FINANCIAL INDEPENENCE

Investing in real estate can lead to financial independence. Oliver, a friend of mine, and a novice but early investor, began his pivotal experiences in 1992. These paved the path to his financial freedom.

Oliver bought a home in Etobicoke for $200,000. He paid down $50,000 and financed the balance. He was working two factory jobs but dreamt of becoming financially independent. As his realtor, I assisted him in finding his first tenant: a jockey. At nights, the home was lively with ladies, liquor and love. This didn't really help in creating an attractive atmosphere for selling the property as a worthwhile investment, and we both learnt this lesson the hard way.

Today, however, having spent the time and having learnt from his mistakes, my friend is financially independent, owning some of the best commercial properties with tenants such as Tim Hortons and Food Basics. He has kept his first investment, that little bungalow in Etobicoke, as a reminder of how dreams can lead to financial independence.

It's been over twenty-seven years since Oliver acquired his first investment property and he's collected around half a million dollars in rental income from that home. That's impressive, considering that he initially invested only $50,000. The home is now worth a staggering $800,000. In about twenty-seven years, he has managed to transform $50,000 to over $1,000,000 in wealth creation by focusing on rental income and capital appreciation.

INCREASE IN NET WORTH:

Current Value of property:		$800,000
Purchase Price:	$200,000	
Capital Appreciation:		$600,000
Rental Income over 25 years:		$500,000

Total Increase in Net Worth:
$1,100,000

The lesson here: *Wealth creation is part of a long-term strategy.*

During those twenty-seven years, Oliver withdrew $400,000 of equity from his little Etobicoke bungalow and used it as down payments on four other residential properties. Today, the rental income from the five properties grosses over $120,000 per year. What's exciting is that this is passive income. Oliver could have pooled his capital into Registered Retirement Savings Plans (RRSPs in Canada) twenty-seven years ago, but that would not have made him financially independent.

Money withdrawn from a retirement plan (in Canada) before retiring and converted into a Registered Retirement Income Plan (RRIF in Canada) is taxable on the entire sum. However, one can refinance a rental property anytime, using the proceeds to continue investing **without paying tax**. Adding up the rental income (not taking any tax implications in consideration) and the recent appreciation of the five properties, he is $2,000,000 wealthier! The difference real estate investing has made in Oliver's financial independence is eye popping, all due to his determination and a little luck. NOTES: A) All figures quoted are Gross. B) Rental Income after allowable expenses to earn such income, is taxable, on an individual or corporate basis, in many jurisdictions.

"Luck", according to Oliver, means "Labor Under Correct Knowledge". Knowledge is acquired over time but, at times, we must leap and learn from our mistakes. Some people are sure-footed in life. They want to make sure that everything is perfect before investing but sometimes those who are sure-footed never leave the shore!

Oliver's success was due to his use of leverage. By using his "lever", he was able to maximize his return. By growing steadily and selecting properties within the guidelines set out above, he minimized his risk.

I am fortunate to have had many teachers like Oliver. Looking back, I had much to learn about real estate, having grown up bare footed on a country farm where financial acumen was as elusive as a needle in a haystack.

LESSONS LEARNED

- Start early, but keep in mind, it's never too late to start
- Consider wealth creation as a long-term strategy. It is the endgame which is most important
- A smart, prudent investor develops the skills needed to anticipate and solve problems before they emerge

1.04 INVESTING IN REAL ESTATE

Investing in real estate is one of the best ways to become wealthy. It is a slow but almost guaranteed path to success, acting as a hedge against inflation. While inflation gradually decreases the buying power of your cash balance, property values gradually appreciate over time in North America (and most western countries). Some may prefer other investments, such as investing in the stock market which is riskier and requires the right skills and knowledge. Real estate on the other hand is easier—just buy, hold and prosper.

TAX ADVANTAGES IN BUYING REAL ESTATE:

1. Ability to write-off the interest portion of a mortgage loan

2. Deducting the cost of maintaining and renovating the rental property

3. Ability to carry-forward losses on the property to be offset against future profits on the same property

4. When you sell the property, the profit (capital gains) is taxed more favorably compared to other sources of income. In addition, some jurisdictions provide for Capital Gains Exemptions. [Consult your Accountant as this varies among jurisdictions and year to year.]

5. Each investment property becomes a passive income stream

LET'S INVEST

The first step is to arrange financing. If you pour half a cup of water into another cup, the total amount of water will not diminish. Your wealth is like that water. You can take some equity from your current home to buy your first investment property. One method of accessing that equity is through a secure line of credit against your home, issued by your bank. This type of loan is called a Home Equity Line of Credit (a "HELOC"). For investment purposes, it is wise to get the maximum HELOC available to capitalize on your equity. The interest payment on the HELOC becomes a tax write-off since you are borrowing for investment purposes.

As an investor, you should not be in a rush. First, choose the location and the size, and consider the upgrades last. Homes that need repairs are usually good investments because once you spruce them up, the value also increases. As mentioned earlier, the best investments are detached homes on large lots in the mature sections of town. Always buy what is easy to sell. Homes that are damaged, in poor locations, have been used as grow-ops, etc., are all examples of what lenders may be unwilling to finance. With grow-ops, for example, even if the house undergoes remedial treatment, it will still have the stigma attached. I have come across instances where the seller had to disclose that the home was a previous grow-op, ultimately affecting the selling price.

All else being equal, it is advantageous to use the same insurance company for your investment. I have experienced situations where the insurer thought that the investment property was the client's residence and denied the claim. When the same insurance company covers both the principal residence and the investment properties, there is a clear distinction established. Having all your insurance with the same company will also give you better negotiating power with that company in terms of discounts.

A good rental property should be one that is easy to both clean and maintain when the current tenant moves. Ceramic tiles and laminate floors are examples of wonderful, easy-to-maintain materials. Once you have considered the property, the next step is to choose the right tenant. Consider that well-kept single-family homes attract excellent tenants.

Over the years, your equity will grow, your mortgage principal will diminish, and your rent receivables will increase. The equity gained over time from that property can be used as a "lever" (down payment) to buy another property in about five to seven years. At retirement, four rental properties, each earning $2,500 per month, will give you a retirement income of $120,000 every year. Not bad!

BUILDING WEALTH

True wealth is built prudently and methodically. With a few rental properties under your belt, small rental increases gradually add up into more positive cash flow.

Here is a living example of what I mean. Let's look back at Oliver's bungalow which he bought for $200,000 in 1992—a top price then! As I mentioned, Oliver invested $50,000 into this property. He then rented it for $1,450 per month. To build equity as fast as possible, Oliver doubled his mortgage payments to the bank. The equity from this little bungalow bought four other properties as well as his financial freedom.

The first rental property is always the most challenging. If you focus on paying down the mortgage, then, in about five to seven years, refinancing that home will pay for another.

Eventually, the two homes will buy four and the four will buy eight. The trick is to build a positive, consistent income stream, not to just own a lot of properties! Like many things in life, quality is more important than quantity. Plan your work and work your plan.

As an investor, always try to buy when everyone is selling. If the market is overheated, the seller has all the options, and then it might be wise to focus on upgrading your current homes. With the upgrades, your tenants will be happier. On a long-term basis, every tenant provides an income stream that will go to work for you. When the market changes, it's time to use the equity from the current rental properties to buy others.

LESSONS LEARNED

- Educate yourself
- Connect with reliable real estate professionals
- Invest the equity in your home to generate more income
- Do your due diligence before investing in a property
- Start small and build on your experience
- A positive cashflow property becomes an asset

SECTION II: STARTING OUT

2.01 YOUR FIRST PURCHASE

Buying your first home is one of the biggest decisions you will ever make. It involves hundreds of thousands of dollars and one bad choice can be financially fatal. Here are a few suggestions to assist you.

THE CONTRACT WITH THE REALTOR

Like an experienced sailor, a prudent and experienced realtor can navigate you across the treacherous, shark-infested waters of real estate.

Your realtor may ask you to sign a Buyer's Representation Agreement. This is a contract that, once signed, is valid for a period and states how the realtor will be compensated. Usually, the realtor is paid by the seller's brokerage but in many instances, it is by the buyer. Review the contract before signing. A realtor's contract with a buyer typically extends for two to three months. Avoid contracts that have longer terms. It is better to renew a contract than to be tied down with the same realtor for a long time.

Ask your realtor to provide a copy of the contract signed and keep the documents well-organized.

KNOW HOW MUCH YOU CAN AFFORD

In a sprawling metropolis with a growing population, such as Toronto, there will always be a demand for homes. What seems expensive today will look like a bargain soon.

With the help of a mortgage broker, you will know how much a lender will provide and how much you will have to finance. Let's assume that you qualify for a mortgage of $500,000. Ask your mortgage broker to work backwards, with the assumption that you buy a home for $500,000, and estimate your monthly payments including mortgage, property taxes, insurance and utilities.

If the payments are too high, ask your mortgage broker to re-work the maximum figure based on a lower mortgage amount. Knowing how much you can afford gives you more buying power. You can now look for homes available within that price range. If you are working from home, you can buy out-of-town where the prices are much more affordable.

BUY SMART

Choose to view homes based first on location, then size, and lastly amenities. Always buy what you feel will be easy to sell if the need arises.

If you are considering a home that requires maintenance fees, such as a condominium apartment or townhome, take into consideration that instead of paying a mortgage plus maintenance fees, it might be better to buy a freehold without the maintenance fees. For example, $500 in monthly condo fees is the same as carrying $100,000 in mortgage at 3.5%. It is a better long-term option because condo fees will increase over time whereas mortgage payments will gradually erode (amortize).

Homes with registered basement apartments are good choices because the projected income from the basement will help you qualify for a higher mortgage and increase your buying power. In addition, the extra income will come in handy and when you are ready to sell, buyers will pay more because of this advantage.

Once you find the home you want, before you finalize the purchase, ask your realtor to inquire whether the seller has a *Seller Property Information Statement.* This is a disclosure statement that the seller may have provided to the realtor. Consider whether the home has major defects and make a well-informed decision based on the disclosure.

You can also request a *History Report* that would provide information on the property, like if it had an insurance claim for fire, flood, sewage back-up, or if the property was ever used as a grow-op from *www.homeverified.com.*

Put away about 1.5% of the purchase price for closing fees. In addition to your down payment, you will need to account for closing costs (type and amount depend on jurisdiction).

CHECKLIST FOR THE FIRST PURCHASE:

☐ Competent Mortgage Broker engaged based on references.

☐ Pre-qualification for mortgage done with a financial institution

☐ All closing costs considered for the purchase:

- o Home Inspection Fees

- o Appraisal Fees

- o Land Transfer Tax (depending on Jurisdiction)

- o Lawyer's Fees

- o Title Insurance and Disbursements

- o HST on CMHC Fees (depending on Jurisdiction).

☐ Budget includes all monthly costs for the property:

- o Municipal Rates and Taxes

- o Condo Fees if applicable

- o Mortgage Payment

- o Utilities (Hydro, Heating, etc.)

- o Contingency for emergencies

2.02 SURVEY ESSENTIALS

A land survey is like a map of the property. Most importantly, it outlines the boundaries of the property. Every property has a street address and a legal description. The survey represents a drawing of the legal description. It helps to define the exact dimensions and boundaries of the property and any easements on it. A land survey is for freehold properties and for parcels of tied lands (POTL) but not for condominiums.

OBTAINING A SURVEY

If you do not have a survey of your property, there are various ways to obtain one. Check with your neighbors on both sides as each survey has the adjacent properties attached to it for reference. Check with the local land registry office or the city or town office.

(In Ontario, you can also buy a copy:

The Ontario Land Surveyors Association website: www.landsurveyrecords.com)

If all else fails, the homeowner can order a new survey of the property by employing a local surveyor. The cost can be upwards of one thousand dollars. Although it is not a requirement, it is important to ask for a copy of the survey when purchasing a property.

EASEMENTS

An easement is a right of use given to someone other than the homeowner. Easements were created in England when homes were built very close to each other. Homeowners required access to take coal for their furnaces along the narrow space, half-owned by each, and the adoption of easements provided a mutually beneficial solution.

A shared driveway between two homes is an example of a modern-day easement where both sets of homeowners benefit from the use of each other's land. A homeowner cannot erect a fence on his portion since it would restrict the other owner's right of access which is granted by the easement. Typically, easements come (i.e., "run") with the land. If the owner sells the property, most easements will remain, granting the new homeowner the right to access.

Properties also have easements for utility companies such as water, gas, hydro, cable and drains. A survey will show these easements. There are instances where a sunroom, a deck or a garden shed is built, and the homeowner later discovers there is an easement which is encumbered by these new additions. In such cases, the homeowner will be required to remove the structure. The expenses and additional work to do so can be avoided by reviewing the survey. Most utility lines run along the road and to the property under the driveway. In some older neighborhoods, this might not be the case.

There are also instances where buyers purchase small homes on a large lot with the belief that they can break down and construct a larger home or build an extension. They may, however, find that there is an easement running through the middle of the lot. Nothing can be built within a certain distance from that easement and that is known as a "setback". In addition, there may be restrictions to the size of the building for that particular property, so always check with the Municipality before proceeding.

As noted above, there are also instances where a fence was previously built over the property boundaries and onto a neighbour's property. It would be costly to tear down and rebuild the fence on the property line. These days, many prospective homeowners elect not to request a copy of the survey because they have purchased title insurance.

TITLE INSURANCE AND LIENS

Title insurance is a type of insurance policy that protects the homeowner from certain losses related to transferring title. This insurance can be purchased at the time of transfer of title to the new owner.

Liens are registered claims against the property. Examples include unpaid debts such as outstanding property taxes from a previous owner or unpaid amounts for services performed on the property, such as the installation of windows or a furnace. Liens may also relate to an encroachment such as a fence or garden shed on a property that is on the neighbour's land and must be removed if the new owner is to take "clear title" of the property. Note that title insurance will not cover costs related to loss in the value of the property because of certain easements. The responsibility is on the buyer (policyholder) to find out.

CHECKLIST FOR SURVEY ESSENTIALS

☐ Survey available and obtained

☐ Easements on the property (done by the buyer's lawyer) if any (like Utility companies) have been investigated

☐ No liens registered and/or are outstanding on the property (done by the buyer's lawyer)

☐ Title insurance coverage purchased on the property (arranged by the buyer's lawyer)

2.03 HOME INSPECTIONS: WORTH IT?

It was a cold winter evening when Sunil and Anita found their perfect home.

The home was recently renovated and there were many bidders. Out of excitement, Sunil and Anita waived the inspection, despite their realtor's recommendation, and submitted a firm offer. They were the lucky ones, or should I say unlucky?

The crocuses were sprouting under heavy rain and melting ice in early spring when Sunil and Anita took possession. From the thaw, water seeped into the basement walls and toxic mold sprouted. Sunil immediately contacted his lawyer but soon realized that he bought the home "as is". The previous owner was not aware of the problem because the ground was frozen, and the basement was dry.

A home inspector would have noticed the crack on the outer wall and, with a moisture meter, would have detected any other problems. The roof was covered with snow at the time of purchase and Sunil did not realize that it was nearing the end of its useable life. The attic was poorly insulated and inadequately ventilated.

After purchasing the property, Anita sat in the living room and admired the open concept design.

It was love at first sight. With more daylight and all the blinds opened, she gazed at the ceiling. There was a small hairline crack that she hadn't noticed before. The previous owner had removed a supporting wall to create the open concept design. Sunil and Anita had no recourse because it was stated in the agreement of purchase and sale that *"the buyer acknowledges, having had the opportunity to inspect the property and understands that upon acceptance of this offer, there shall be a binding agreement of purchase and sale between the buyer and seller."*

If you are buying a home that was recently renovated, check if there was a building permit, especially when walls were removed to create an open concept design.

BENEFITS OF A HOME INSPECTION

Home inspections may not reveal all the problems and defects, but an efficient inspector will discover major issues. Inspections usually take between two to three hours and if possible, the buyer should accompany the inspector. A good inspector will give maintenance advice to the buyer during the inspection and if they are a new homeowner, may help alleviate some of their new-home jitters.

Most inspections start with the outside of the home and finish in the basement, checking for foundation cracks, soil gradient, receptacles, vents, and anything visually defective (a "patent"). Home inspectors will snap photos of any defect and comment on it in their inspection report.

Inspectors will check for moisture levels in the home and, with an infra-red camera, can detect whether there is heat loss or even insect or vermin infestation.

In multiple offers where the buyer has a better chance of securing the home by going firm, it is better to have an inspection done prior to the offer presentation date. This is becoming increasingly common and there are occasions where sellers have an inspection prepared for interested buyers prior to offer presentations. This saves time and allows the seller to receive offers that are not subject to inspections. Buyers can make an offer based on the report.

HOME INSPECTION FOR CONDOS

Inspections are also advisable for condo townhomes and freehold properties. With condominium apartments, it depends, because there is not much to inspect, since common areas such as the roof, underground garage and elevators are the responsibility of the Condominium Corporation (management). While the condominium owner is responsible for the interior space which would include the walls, plumbing for kitchen and washrooms, some electrical work and the appliances, there may be Condo Bylaws that impose restrictions on certain elements of the apartment. For example: curtains might have to meet certain standards and the structure of the apartment might be unchangeable. If the seller has made changes without permission, the buyer could be stuck with the cost of reverting to the original design.

Inspectors usually charge less for condominium apartment inspections.

Most buyers conduct a home inspection only after their financing has been arranged. If the inspection reveals major deficiencies, then the buyer can terminate the deal and have their deposit returned. In many instances, the buyer can re-negotiate with the seller. It is a good practice to inspect the appliances and note the make, model, and serial number at the time of inspection to ensure these are the same appliances that are turned over when the sale is closed.

INSPECTION FOR NEW HOMES

New homes should also be inspected. There are many cases where problems already exist, for example a floor joist could be further apart than the Ontario Building Code allows. Although new homes are covered under the Tarion Warranty in Ontario (check the Warranty in your jurisdiction), certain ("latent") defects can remain undetected.

Home inspections will not reveal every defect and there is no guarantee that problems will not arise after closing. Buying a home to nest in is an expensive venture and it should be inspected. After all, it will become your nest egg.

CHECKLIST FOR HOME INSPECTIONS

- ☐ Home inspection built into the Offer to Purchase
- ☐ In the case of a condominium apartment, Condo Bylaws not contravened
- ☐ Accredited home inspector contracted
- ☐ Appointment made to be present at the inspection
- ☐ Report on the inspection carefully analyzed and minor and major flaws explained
- ☐ Final decision to purchase made only after the report is analyzed

2.04 BUYING NEW

When buying new, plan for the next five to ten years. Will the family structure change? Will there be additions to the family? Take into consideration additional parking for an extra car if needed. Take a realistic look at your financing.

Choose a location that is right for you. Always consider schools and commuting time. Consider changes in lifestyle. Seniors may want a bedroom and a full bath on the main floor while a young couple may want more space to raise a family.

BEFORE MAKING AN OFFER TO A BUILDER:

1. Check the builder's reputation

2. Talk to the neighbours already living there

3. Check with the local Home Builders Association (if the builder is a member) to assess the builder's reputation

4. Check with the Better Business Bureau (BBB) for valid complaints against the company.

5. Consider the builder's after-sales service

6. Know what is covered by your warranty

WATCH OUT FOR HIDDEN COSTS

Unlike a resale, new home purchases can be daunting. Hidden costs cannot be added to the mortgage and must be paid upfront. In addition to the down payment, you might be responsible to pay the following in advance:

- Development fees
- Deposit verification fees
- Builder's mortgage discharge fees
- Education lot levy
- Builder's legal fees
- New home warranty fees
- Water, gas, and hydro meter fees
- Other costs that might be applicable

Always keep in mind that the salesperson at the builder's office is working for the builder and may not be able to represent the buyer. It is better to have your own realtor accompany you. Unlike condominiums, which have a 10-day cooling off period, purchasing freehold properties may be non-refundable. However, some builders will allow the buyers forty-eight hours. Make the contract conditional upon your lawyer's approval.

UPGRADES

Most people fall in love with the model home but fail to keep in mind that **almost everything in the model home is an upgrade**. Budget accordingly and only choose upgrades necessary in the short term. Builders usually make the highest profit on upgrades.

Choose upgrades that are easy and cost effective to do at the time of purchase such as higher ceilings, larger basement windows and separate basement entrances. Upgrades such as thicker carpets and granite countertops can wait.

Banks will finance the property at base value and may not cover the cost of upgrades. The closing cost and cost for upgrades may be out-of-pocket expenses and need to be included in your budget.

When buying new, expect delays and plan for this eventuality and its impact on your financing and current living accommodation. Builders will give adequate notices if there is a delay. The contract may have a "Critical Date" and if that date passes, the buyer can agree with the new closing date and seek compensation from the Builder for the delay or, in the event none is forthcoming, can opt out of the deal. About one week before completion, the builder will schedule a pre-inspection.

PRE-CLOSING INSPECTION

I've accompanied many of my clients to their pre-closing inspection. Usually, a representative from the builder will attend. In almost all the inspections, the "builder's inspector" would inspect the painter's flaws and stick pieces of papers on things that would need to be redone. I found that the buyers were fixated on the wall pointing out minor painting flaws to the builder's representative and, in the process, would unintentionally change their focus.

During the pre-closing inspection, check if the home is built according to the plan. Look for imperfections and defects. I have seen it all: new homes without insulation in the attics, toilets that were not anchored and missing towel racks and dryer vents.

Have the home inspected by a professional inspector. After the inspection, the builder will give you an inspection sheet to sign stating that you have reviewed the home and that you are satisfied with everything except the defects (if any) listed in the statement. If you missed something and it is not covered by the warranty, the builder can refuse to fix it.

New homes are protected under a private third-party warranty (in some jurisdictions the warranty is administered by a government or quasi government agency). The warranty will cover deposit insurance, protect against faulty workmanship and defective materials but may not cover everything. Before the warranty expires, get another home inspection done so that if there are any defects, you are covered.

CHECKLIST FOR BUYING

☐ Extensive research done on the builder

☐ The new home will meet our future needs as our family expands or changes

☐ Emotion has been taken out of selecting upgrades

☐ Hidden costs were budgeted

☐ The pre-inspection was carefully evaluated

☐ A Home Inspector was engaged (if needed)

2.05 CONDO LIVING

A condominium (condo) is defined as a building where the units are individually owned while common areas such as the roof, passageway(s) and elevator(s), etc. are owned by a condominium corporation which represents all the owners jointly. Joint ownership imposes rules, and all condos have bylaws that must be followed.

A condo lifestyle can be alluring. There is no need to worry about the day-to-day maintenance that comes with owning a home — shoveling snow, cutting the grass, and fixing roof shingles. Modern condominiums also offer high-caliber amenities, from theaters to car wash stations. Condo living is considered as *breezy*, but, as with any real estate investment, caution is necessary. Sometimes a breeze can mean that a storm is brewing.

Since the COVID-19 pandemic, families have been moving away from the GTA [Greater Toronto Area] to smaller Ontario communities. This trend will continue as more people can and will want to work from home. Many are leaving the confined space of condos and relocating to more affordable detached homes outside of the GTA to raise a family.

Humans are social creatures, and it cannot be overstated how much we depend on each other to survive. It is no surprise, therefore, that a pandemic such as Covid has and will continue to affect our lives in many ways. Similar outbreaks such as SARS and MERS are indicators that in a fast-moving world, it is difficult to control the spread of germs. While condominium living is affordable and has amenities such as pools and gyms, COVID-19 has taught us that if we are caught in an elevator with a potentially contagious individual, it could be detrimental to our health. While there will still be an appetite for condos because of affordability and convenience, the pandemic has highlighted the tradeoffs that come with sharing space. After all, the best investment on earth is the earth itself.

HOW CONDOMINIUMS FUNCTION

The law stipulates that management must provide a report that lays out the state of all the common areas and the maintenance cost of future repairs. For example, if the roof needs to be changed in five years at a cost of half a million, then that money must be saved in a Reserve Fund.

Condominiums have a monthly association or maintenance fees which partly gets held in a reserve fund for future repairs, and the other portion is used for day-to-day management. The Bylaws of the condominium corporation, along with the reserve fund study, are part of a special report called the *Status Certificate*. A prospective buyer's lawyer will review the status certificate to ensure that the condominium's reserve fund is adequate. The Certificate reveals any concerns of the condominium, for example if there are any pending lawsuits or projected increases in maintenance fees.

It is paramount to attend management meetings and know what is happening. I remember an incident where the president of a condominium used his influence to elect his friends. The funds were mismanaged and eventually every unit owner had to pay an additional special assessment fee of $36,000 (i.e., on top of usual maintenance fees) to cover the cost of repairs. Banks refused to give mortgages on new purchases and with the looming problem, many owners decided to sell. Prices plummeted.

Condominiums have insurance but this is not adequate for the suite owner. The building insurance covers what happens outside the suite (i.e., to the "common elements"). A broken washer hose for example, can result in water damages to many units and the cost of repairs could be steep due to resulting property damage. Owners should have adequate liability and content insurance. Most insurance companies will provide special "condominium insurance" packages targeted to the risks of condo living. Consider having an insurance broker find you a condominium insurance package which includes coverage for both property damage as well as general liability.

Any plan to modernize the suite requires approval from management. Every condominium has rules on renovations. Some condominiums even have stipulations on the type of materials that can be used. In an adult lifestyle building, for example, the bylaws only allow for carpeting. Typically, construction can only be done at certain times, minimizing the disturbance to others. Removal of construction materials requires the use of the elevators where the bylaws require a potential damage deposit.

Anything that is considered as common elements should not be tampered with and that includes the unit doors. For example, installing a door stopper on the entry door could result in the condominium management removing it and billing the owner for the cost of removal and repairs. It is imperative that buyers review the Status Certificate before purchasing so that they are familiar with what they can or cannot do.

For those who are currently living in a condo, know your management and remember you have a right to oversee the management as well. Attend all the meetings and if there is a pressing issue, address it. Condo living can be carefree when residents care about the well-being of other unit owners. Get involved in the day-to-day management; talk to other unit owners and develop a collective pride of ownership. A well-managed building with a strong reserve of funds and low maintenance fees has many advantages.

PURCHASING YOUR PERFECT SUITE

Like buying a house, you should obtain a mortgage pre-approval before beginning your search. A pre-approval will provide the price range you can afford and let you know your buying power. After pre-approval, check out neighborhoods first and then look at the condominiums within your price range.

Visit each building and compare suite sizes and amenities. A modern building, for example, with great amenities, would be more expensive and the maintenance fees would be higher than buildings with less amenities.

If the building is run down and the common areas are dirty, then it would be less attractive to prospective buyers and with time, the maintenance fees will climb. An unattractive building with high condominium fees is a recipe for disaster. In Toronto, I have seen condominiums that sold in 1989 for $134,000 that sold recently for under $50,000 because of that reason.

Once you find the suite you want to buy, do your homework. Look at the view and make sure you like what you see. Suites that overlook garage entrances and garbage pickup areas are not desirable and would be more difficult to sell when you plan to move. Buy in premium, live in premium and sell in premium.

When purchasing a condominium suite, your lawyer must review the Bylaws, which vary from building to building. Failing to comply with the

Bylaws can result in stiff financial penalties, or even eviction. One of the bylaws, for example, can address the quiet enjoyment of all occupants and addresses noise complaints. I recall an incident where a few friends got together for a social gathering and the neighbours were disturbed. The board slapped the unit owner with a $750 penalty. Another incident involved an owner violating a Bylaw where pets were not allowed. A buyer who does not familiarize himself with the bylaws of his condominium will suffer the consequences.

PRE-BUILT CONDOMINIUMS

Since pre-built condominiums may take a few years to complete, it allows you to save up more for the down payment. The condo value may increase substantially and sometimes the price increase dwarfs the down payment. Newly built condos will typically have lower condo fees compared to an older resale and you have many customizable choices, such as size, floors, etc.

However, while there are many advantages of buying pre-built, there is always the other side of the coin to consider. Pre-built condominiums can take years to finalize and during that time the buyer can get tied up in large deposits with the builder without receiving any interest, unless enshrined in government legislation. Unlike resales, you cannot see exactly what you are buying and when bought from a plan, the actual unit built might not meet your expectation when you see it in person.

CHECKLIST FOR CONDO LIVING

- ☐ Mortgage pre-approval obtained
- ☐ Checklist prepared for features desired
- ☐ Checklist prepared for comparison of potential purchased units
- ☐ Amenities in the condo meet expectations and requirements
- ☐ Status Certificate professionally reviewed by competent authority
- ☐ Bylaws reviewed to determine owner's obligations, liabilities, and responsibilities
- ☐ Cost of insurance policy for contents and liability evaluated

2.06 THE OFFER AND CLOSING

Timing is important. Omar and Nadine fell in love with a home, but it was already sold conditionally to another buyer, subject to that buyer obtaining financing by midnight. Omar and Nadine submitted a Conditional Offer to the seller in case the previous offer could not be finalized. It was one minute after midnight when the previous buyer's realtor provided the seller's realtor with the waiver for financing. However, since the previous offer expired at midnight, Omar and Nadine got the property.

THE OFFER TO PURCHASE

An offer is an agreement to purchase a property under specific conditions. This agreement is time sensitive and contains specific contractual deadlines.

The first deadline is in the "irrevocability" clause, typically stating that the person presenting the offer cannot revoke it until after the time specified in the agreement. I recall an incident in which the seller gave the buyer a specific deadline to firm-up the offer to purchase but then changed his mind and decided not to sell. However, the buyer decided to accept the offer during the timeframe in which it was still irrevocable. As a result, the seller could not escape his legal obligation and had to proceed with the sale.

As a buyer, it is in your best interests to make the timeframe for offer acceptance as short as reasonably possible because it weeds out sellers who are not serious. Long irrevocability timeframes give the seller the ability to seek alternative buyers while your money sits around. If the offer is not accepted within the given period, the offer expires, and the process can start all over again.

In many instances, a realtor will prepare an offer on a case-by-case basis depending on the client's specific needs. That said, there are some common things to pay attention to in any given offer.

With respect to the deposit, this money is held in a trust account by the seller's real estate brokerage or lawyer until the closing date. The initial deposit should be made when an offer is accepted. The buyer often has a window of twenty-four hours to arrange for the deposit. If the deposit is not made, the agreement can be voided. Many buyers have their funds locked into RRSP or mutual funds. In such cases, it is critical that the Sales Agreement states that the buyer will make the deposit by a certain date.

Most offers are subject to financing and inspection. A buyer may be pre-approved for a mortgage, but the borrower cannot arrange a mortgage unless there is an accepted offer because the mortgage is assigned to (and secured by) the property rather than the buyer.

An inspection should be completed within a given timeframe. In most cases, an inspection is carried out within five business days from the date that the offer has been accepted. If the inspection is not performed within the allotted time, the offer becomes void. Keep in mind, however, that the buyer reserves the right to remove a condition within said allotted time, making the offer firm and binding on all parties.

Once the conditions (such as obtaining financing or performing an inspection) are satisfied, a written notice of fulfillment from the buyer is required. This notice must be signed by the buyer and sent to the seller's realtor during the specified time. The seller must sign an acknowledgement that he or she has received it.

Before the closing date, the buyer's lawyer will conduct a title search. This is the history of the property. The title search can reveal the following:

- Information regarding all previous owners

- Whether or not the sellers have the legal right to sell the property (i.e., whether they have "title")

- Other information such as mortgages or liens (claims) registered against the property (i.e., any "encumbrance" on title)

The buyer's lawyer has a timeframe to research the title. This is known as the period of "Due

Diligence". The deadline for conducting the research is called the "Requisition Date". Within that time, the buyer's solicitor must send a list of things to the seller's lawyer to be addressed. If it is not done before the requisition date, then those defects can go with the property.

To register a mortgage on a property, the lender requires a "Clean Title" and if the title has defects, the lender can refuse to finance the property. This is serious because the buyer may not be able to close the transaction and can be sued by the seller. Requisition dates should be set about two weeks before the final date, but the buyer's lawyer should conduct a search much earlier. If there is a problem with the title, the seller's lawyer needs time to address it.

Regarding the closing date, it's the date when ownership/title and money change hands. Many steps must be taken simultaneously:

1. The lending entity (for the buyer) must transfer the loaned amount to the lawyer's trust account.
2. Property insurance must be arranged.
3. All conditions specified in the offer confirmed as being met.

This must be done when the Land Title Registry Office is open. The Registry is a government agency that transfers title in the property from the seller to the buyer. [The name of the office varies from jurisdiction to jurisdiction. Check with yours]. Time is critical. If the deal cannot be finalized on time because of a delay by the buyer, then the seller can suffer a significant financial blow, especially if his purchase of another property hinges on this transaction. Sometimes many transactions are on the same thread. A seller who sold might have bought as well, and the domino effect can be financially disastrous.

CHECKLIST FOR THE OFFER AND CLOSING:

- ☐ The irrevocability clause is the deadline set for the offer/ acceptance of the sale/ purchase of the property

- ☐ The Offer To Purchase includes:
    - ○ The amount of the deposit
    - ○ Financing arrangements
    - ○ Inspection of the property
    - ○ The title search date
    - ○ The closing date for the transaction

2.07 CLOSING COSTS

When buying a home, in addition to the down payment, buyers must pay closing costs. Closing costs are the amount of additional money buyers will need to transfer the home into their name and can vary from one transaction and jurisdiction to another.

THE IMPACT OF CLOSING COSTS

Home inspections are optional but recommended. A home inspection can cost as low as $250 for a condo or can be several hundred dollars for other homes. It is a small investment to obtain peace of mind for possibly the largest and most important purchase you will make.

Financing is complex. If your down payment is at least 20%, your credit is clean, and your income is adequate, then it is not expensive to finance. If your down payment is less than 20%, the mortgage might need to be insured by an institution in your jurisdiction (in Canada, usually by Canada Mortgage and Housing Corporation — CMHC) for the bank's protection. The banks would add the premium to the mortgage.

The insurance premium may cost as much as 4% of the mortgage for buyers whose down payment is only 5%. Although the bank lends the premium to the buyer, there might be a sales tax cost (in Canada, Harmonized Sales Tax — HST) on the premium. There might also be a processing fee.

If you are using a mortgage broker or a secondary lender, then there might be other fees such as mortgage broker fees, lender's fees, and finder's fees. In some situations, the buyer may need two mortgages and the fees can escalate. Most banks and financial institutions will also need an appraisal done at the buyer's expense before lending. Always ask for a Mortgage Commitment Letter before you remove your financing condition. The commitment letter will disclose all the fees associated with the transaction.

In many instances there is an interest adjustment date. Mortgage payment is due at the end of the month and if the transaction closes in the middle of the month, then the interest for the remaining period must be paid upfront.

Land transfer tax might be applicable (in Ontario is also payable when a title to a property is transferred—check with applicability in your jurisdiction). First-time buyers will benefit from some exemptions.

If you are selling and buying, then consider commissions plus sales tax if applicable in your jurisdiction (in Canada HST applies) on the commission paid to sell your home.

For newly built homes, there might be other charges to consider:

- New home warranty
- Education lot levy
- Grading fees
- Tree planting fees
- Fees for water, gas, and hydro meters
- Survey
- Builder's mortgage discharge fee
- Deposit verification fee

LEGAL FEES

Legal fees must be paid upon closing. Lawyers assist the banks in the preparation and recording of legal documents and transfer the property to the buyer. Lawyer fees vary from one attorney to another. In addition to lawyer fees, buyers must pay for disbursements — certain expenses like registering a mortgage, etc., incurred by the lawyer. There are other closing costs such as that to obtain title insurance, fire insurance, the tax certificate, courier, and photocopying charges. Always ask your lawyer for a statement of adjustment. It explains in detail how your money is spent.

There can be other hidden costs. For example, if the seller paid the property tax for the whole year, then the buyer will be required to adjust accordingly.

To discharge a variable mortgage, the cost is the greater of three months' interest or the interest rate differential for the remainder of the term.

CHECKLIST FOR CLOSING COSTS

- ☐ Home Inspection completed
- ☐ Mortgage insurance arranged
- ☐ Items budgeted for:
  - ○ Mortgage broker/ lender and finder fees
  - ○ Property appraisal fees
  - ○ Land transfer tax
  - ○ New home buyer fees (if applicable)
  - ○ HST [Canadian jurisdictions]
  - ○ Upgrades
  - ○ Title insurance
  - ○ Fire insurance
  - ○ Tax certificate
  - ○ Lawyer's fees
  - ○ Property tax adjustment
  - ○ Interest adjustment
  - ○ Real estate commission
  - ○ Mortgage discharge fees if selling your home

SECTION III: CREATING WEALTH

3.01 ESSENTIAL ELEMENTS: INVESTING

WHERE TO BEGIN

The best deals usually come from the worst problems. Problems can be opportunities waiting to be unwrapped.

    1.   Keep your emotion out of the equation when purchasing. Not because you *fell in love* with the property makes it the best deal. To make your purchase recession-proof, you must show a small profit from the first day. However, keep in mind it's possible that underperforming assets could have room to grow and might make worthwhile investments. (More on this later).

    2.   Buy mid-range rental homes—these homes often appeal to first-time buyers since they make decent rentals, they can be easily rented to the average working-class family and the property taxes and utilities are reasonable.

    3.   Start by identifying an area that you would like to invest in. Visit all the properties currently on the market in that area. Look for distressed properties in the neighborhood. For example, the outside appearance of the home might need sprucing up. You can approach the neighbours and inquire about the reasons

behind the condition. It never hurts to be well informed.

4. Learn to conduct a quick inspection. Look at the major things such as the roof, windows, electrical panel, and furnace. Walk around the outside and look for settlement cracks and water leakage. It might be difficult at first but the more often you do it the more you will excel at it. Later, if you purchase the home, you can hire an inspector to conduct a thorough inspection as a condition of purchase.

CHECKLIST FOR INVESTING

- ☐ List of criteria for a property to invest in
- ☐ Would produce the highest return with the minimum of investment
- ☐ Located in an area with rental in demand
- ☐ Property is mid-range in value and has rental potential
- ☐ Property passes a quick inspection
- ☐ Passes a more in-depth inspection by a competent third-party authority (House Inspector).

3.02 DON'T ATTEMPT IT ALL

To win a good game of hockey, we must not only recruit the best players but also consider synergy. Similarly, the team players you select when you embark on building your investment portfolio in real estate can make or break you.

When it comes time to perform specialized functions, it is best to outsource your time and energy to experts. Your time is money in the sense of opportunity cost. Be careful that you are not saving cents while losing dollars. If you are not adept at a particular task, delegate to the appropriate professional. Spend your time wisely instead, searching for and managing a better investment property.

CRITERIA FOR PROFESSIONALS

- Get references from friends and relatives
- Contact several people in the field
- Get multiple quotes
- Check credentials and ensure trades people are appropriately registered
- Don't pay up front

- Make payments based on % of completion

- Consider arranging for a small "holdback" in case of problems encountered after project completion

- Check the company's BBB rating (A rating from The Better Business Bureau which gives an idea how the business deals with customers)

- Have a contract in writing

- Ask for a copy of the contractor's insurance in event of any accidents.

- For commercial contractors, consider having the contractor add you as an "Additional Insured" to their policy

PROPERTY MANAGERS

As your portfolio grows, you might think of retaining the services of a property manager. A good property management company can free up a lot of your time spent on mundane tasks. With a good property manager, your time is freed up for more cost-efficient functions while they handle the day-to-day operation of the property. They can act as a buffer between you and the tenants and can collect rent and provide proper book-keeping service. Property management fees are also considered as a rental expense against any income, for tax purposes.

When choosing a property manager, make sure your property manager specializes in residential rentals. In commercial projects, the cost to manage the property is paid by the tenants. Read over the contracts very carefully and insert a clause which states that you can cancel at any time at your sole discretion if not pleased with their services.

It is common practice for property managers to open separate accounts for each client. However, some may choose to pool all their clients' money into one account. You should therefore use a property management company that manages your investment in a separate account.

CHECKLIST FOR OUTSIDE HELP

☐ Due diligence completed

    o   Alternatives investigated

    o   Multiple quotes obtained

    o   References checked (BBB or other)

☐ Written agreement or contract on hand

☐ Payment based on percentage of completion

☐ Copy of their liability insurance obtained

☐ Funds accounted for separately if a Property Manager service obtained

3.03 CREATING A FINANCIAL PLAN

A good financial plan gives you a bird's eye view of the project where you can estimate the Rate of Return on the property. The plan must provide a clear projection of monthly expenses as well as the amount of potential rental income. Once prepared, you can determine whether the investment makes financial sense.

Every property you purchase should have a financial plan. The plan should include the following:

- Purchase price

- Borrowing cost

- Monthly payments including:

    - Mortgage

    - Property taxes

    - Insurance

    - Budget for potential repairs

- Allowance for unanticipated repairs, vacancy, and bad debts

CHECK RENTAL RATES IN THE AREA

Once you have an idea of the monthly carrying cost, you need to gauge the rental income you can generate. A realtor can assist.

Another option is to put a few rental ads on social media before purchasing in the area to gauge interest. Doing so can help establish the demand in the area based on the number of inquiries. If you find a good potential tenant, you could then go ahead and find a suitable home for them.

Sometimes an adequate Rate of Return is not possible, but the home still has good growth potential in terms of its capital appreciation. To become financially free, look at the longer term. Over the years the value of the property will increase, the mortgage amount will decrease, and the rent will go up.

CALCULATING YOUR RATE OF RETURN

Rate of Return (RoR) (often referred to as "ROI" — Return on Investment in Finance), is the net gain or loss on an investment over a specified time-period, expressed as a percentage of the investment's initial cost. This tool is important to analyze the outcome before a transaction, keeping in mind that at the end of the day, the objective is to make a small profit.

Keep the following in mind when calculating the RoR:

1. A negative RoR does not mean that a property is a bad investment. Maybe the property is in a great location and the value can climb substantially over time. However, too many investment properties with negative cash flow can become a disaster unless you are buying land for long term and have the resources to carry the shortfall.

2. The highest Rate of Return for all the properties being considered is clearly the one to focus on if your portfolio has limited funds to invest.

3. A positive Rate of Return is not necessarily a good investment. It is only a good investment when compared to the Rate of Return for other comparable investment opportunities, and if it is higher.

4. Repayment of the Principal on a mortgage, is not featured into the calculation.

The formula to calculate the rate of return is:

(Annual Income - annual expense) divided by the amount of money initially invested

CHECKLIST FOR A FINANCIAL PLAN

☐   Financial plan drawn up

☐ Potential rental income/cash inflow determined

☐ Expenses/cash outflow considered

☐ Rate of Return calculated

☐ Rate of Return is an acceptable level (compared to other investment vehicles)

3.04 MAKING NET WORTH WORK

Robert Kiyosaki, the author of *Rich Dad Poor Dad*, talks about the millionaire mindset where two children received an inheritance of $40,000 each. They both buy a new car with their inheritance. One pays cash for it while the other takes dealer's financing and invests the $40,000 in a rental property that costs $400,000. After five years, they both sell their cars for $10,000 but the one with the investment property's portfolio goes up by 10%, giving her an additional $40,000 while her brother remains saddled with a quickly depreciating asset.

MAKING YOUR NET WORTH WORK FOR YOU

Net worth is defined as your total assets less your total liabilities. When applying for either a loan or a mortgage, every financial institution will ask for a Balance Sheet to assess the risk of lending to you. Making this net worth work for you is important if you are trying to increase your wealth. The difference between being well off and seriously wealthy is the relationship between you and your money. Ask yourself, do you just work for your money, or does your money work for you?

Consider, for example, that a home is worth $700,000 and the homeowners have paid off their mortgage in full. They are now ecstatic about being mortgage free. In this case, the owner has worked to pay off the $700,000 but the money is not being put to work!

Arrange a secure line of credit against the property. Setting up a secure line of credit on a mortgage-free home will protect it against fraud. Identity theft is on the rise and one can assume another person's identity, apply for a loan against the home and move the proceeds offshore. A secure line of credit is like a mortgage and since the lender is secured on the title, the lender must be informed if someone wants to use the property to secure a loan.

Once you have money available to invest, it is important to choose the right type of investment. Take myself for example; a banker promised to double my money in just four years. He claimed to be an expert in the stock market and that he had helped many clients like me in the past. Four years later, I cashed out, salvaging only a quarter of what I invested. The mistake I made was choosing the wrong person to assist me. I also did not take the time to educate myself in the field I wanted to invest in.

Investing in real estate is one of the best ways to build wealth. Why not use some of the money from a line of credit to invest in a second home? On average, house prices double every seven to ten years. The recent low-interest rate environment during the COVID-19 pandemic appears to have accelerated this due to high demand and limited supply.

Preserving and growing wealth requires discipline. It is essential that you research the field thoroughly before investing. Solicit help from professionals and schedule interviews with them. Test the waters before plunging into an investment. Hindsight is 20/20 and we all become more educated the second time around. Good business professionals never make instant decisions. They allow at least twenty-four hours to pass before committing. Building wealth is simple. Spend less and invest more. Over time, your wealth will grow exponentially.

GOING FORWARD—POTENTIAL PITFALLS

Mickey took the equity from his home and went prospecting for gold in South America. A year later, he filed for bankruptcy. Mickey never did his research and, like a fish, went after the shiniest lure dangling in the water. However, not all that glitters is gold! Careful research is important. While it is important to learn from one's mistakes, when it comes to wealth preservation, always try to learn from mistakes made by others.

CHECKLIST FOR UTILIZING NET WORTH

☐ Balance Sheet prepared and net worth calculated. [An accountant can help with this process]

- ☐ Line of Credit obtained from financial institution, using the above

- ☐ Professional help (such as a real estate broker, an accountant, and financial advisers) enlisted.

- ☐ Alternatives evaluated

- ☐ Following considered:

  - o The degree of risk involved

  - o The rate of return

- ☐ Best investment selected to maximize Rate of Return.

3.05 ADVICE ON MORTGAGES

The objective is to borrow money at the cheapest rate, thereby keeping your carrying cost at a minimum.

When the carrying cost is low, profitability increases. Shop around for rates because even a half percentage point difference can result in substantial savings over the long haul. In addition to mortgage rates, there are many other things to look out for. For example, simply by locking your HELOC [Home Equity Line of Credit] like a closed mortgage will result in a lower interest rate when compared to leaving it open.

Most residential investment properties require a 20% down payment. Use "A" lenders such as chartered banks, if possible. These lenders are more regulated and easily accessible. Once your financial institution approves your mortgage, you'll be given a *Mortgage Commitment Letter.*

The Mortgage Commitment Letter may have conditions you will need to satisfy before the mortgage is granted, one of which might submission of an Appraisal Report on the investment property. (In most cases, the lender will do his own assessment of the property.) Make sure that all the lenders' conditions are met so that the mortgage is secured. This will ensure a smooth transaction when the deal finally closes.

When choosing a mortgage, some will prefer a long-term fixed interest rate while others may consider a long-term variable rate. Some investors prefer the long-term variable rate with an option to lock in. The variable rate is usually lower than the fixed rate and a borrower can pay down the principal rapidly and build more equity to be reinvested. Since the aim is to buy, hold and profit, some investors choose to double their monthly payment and reduce the amortization drastically, thereby increasing their equity to reinvest.

When arranging a mortgage, always look at the Mortgage Disclosure Statements. A Mortgage Disclosure Statement will tell the borrower about the cost involved in borrowing. This statement varies from one lender to the next. For example, one lender charged $20,000 to break a mortgage that has an outstanding balance of $268,000 with a monthly payment of $1,163. These costs, the lender could argue, are for reinvestment purposes. It was clearly written in the Mortgage Disclosure statement, but the borrower did not notice it when he signed for the mortgage.

Financing is an important aspect in investment. There are many different mortgage options available. While having the lowest interest rate is helpful, the terms of the mortgage contract must be reviewed.

SELLER TAKE-BACK MORTGAGES

A Seller Take-back-Mortgage is one where the seller chooses to become the lender. In some cases, it can be beneficial to both parties. In other cases, it can be dangerous.

Mikhail bought a commercial property where there were environmental problems with the land. The lender refused to finance the property because of the environmental impact. Mikhail had a substantial down payment of 33%. The seller agreed to do a take-back mortgage for 66% of the purchase price for a term of two years. After a careful review, Mikhail decided to opt out of the deal. The reason was that after two years, the seller's take-back mortgage would become due. If Mikhail could not find a new lender, then the seller could exercise power of sale and Mikhal could lose the property. On the other hand, the seller can renew the mortgage at a much higher interest rate with harsher terms.

A Seller Take-back Mortgage is considered a private mortgage where the seller lends the money directly to the buyer. Perhaps the seller bought the property many years ago and is now looking for an exit strategy. It's also possible that the seller is looking for a steady cash flow or trying to defer some of the capital gains tax payable. In some instances, the seller will fund the entire mortgage and hold the property as the security.

An investor can benefit from a Seller Take-back Mortgage because of the lower interest rate they can negotiate. The investor can also tie up less of their own money since the seller is looking for a steady flow of income. The lower interest rate in turn can increase the rate of return on the investment for the buyer.

If the mortgage is a high-ratio mortgage (i.e., under 20% down), the investor does not have to pay an insurance premium, as they would have if taken from a conventional source. Over the long haul, this will benefit both parties.

CHECKLIST FOR MORTGAGES

☐ Mortgage commitment obtained from financial institution

☐ All conditions of the mortgage commitment are satisfied BEFORE making a firm offer

☐ A long-term variable rate with an option to lock in the rate negotiated (unless a long-term fixed rate is more advantageous in the current market—e.g., you expect interest rates to rise significantly in the next few years).

☐ Increased mortgage payments budgeted

☐ Mortgage Disclosure Statement from the lender examined for onerous conditions

☐ Seller Take-back Mortgage explored for advantages

3.06 PUTTING HOME EQUITY TO USE

Homeowners became wealthier during the COVID-19 pandemic. Home prices surged and continued to climb in 2021. Homeowners are in a unique position because they can use some of their equity to plant seeds for further financial growth. Benjamin Franklin said that an investment in knowledge pays the best interest. These transforming ideas can quantum leap your net worth if you manage your risk.

Use some of the equity to buy an investment property. With inflation and limited supply of materials, construction is becoming expensive, and in turn, home prices are appreciating. Currently, for every home available for sale, there are about six buyers. A two-family home can be rented annually for $40,000. This is called passive income because the person does not have to actively work for it. Gradually, it's best to replace active income with passive. Toronto will continue to be a hotspot for immigrants, meaning demand for housing will only increase over time. In the long term, prices will trend upwards, the remaining balance on the mortgage will decrease and if we add up the rent collected over the years, returns begin to add up to financial freedom. To put icing on the cake, the interest on the money borrowed for investment is tax deductible.

The equity in your property can also be used for less speculative ventures. For example, debt consolidation may be able to immediately save you money. Sai, for example, has a total of $29,000 in credit card debts, paying $1,160 monthly. He chooses to increase his mortgage by $29,000 and pay off his debts. His monthly payment drops to $115. Fitzroy, on the other hand, took out a second mortgage on his home for $100,000 at 12% interest in 2018, paying $1053 monthly. Initially, the first mortgagor had refused to lend him the additional $100,000 because, at that time, the property loan-to-value ratio (a ratio lenders use to calculate risk) was too high. With the recent price growth, the loan-to-value ratio dropped significantly. Fitzroy managed to increase the first mortgage and paid off the second. By doing so, he now saves $653 monthly.

Many families with adult children can use this idea. It's the perfect time to give adult children a head-start in life. Arthur's parents took $100,000 from their family home to help Arthur. He used the money as a down payment on a newly built condo that would be ready in five years. Arthur estimates that he can double his initial investment in five years. He can then use the proceeds of sale to catapult him into a home. Arthur now has a goal to work towards. His aim is to repay his parents in five years. Another family took money from their family home and opened a thriving take-out restaurant, creating employment for themselves. Since they borrowed money from their family home to invest in their business, the interest on that portion became tax deductible.

With prices so high, consider whether money is best spent moving or, instead, renovating or extending your current home. With COVID-19, many families are working from home and require more space. It is easy to add a second level on a bungalow because the building foundation is already there. Find a good contractor who can point you in the right direction. Once that is done, get an estimate. Always over-budget by ten to fifteen percent for the unexpected. With an architectural drawing, building permit and a good contractor, you are on your way. If you are modernizing, the quality of materials can make a big difference. The cost of installation usually remains the same. It's best to buy your own materials and ask the contractor to quote you on labor. Remember to ensure that contractors have the appropriate insurance coverage.

Building a secondary suite is a good idea. The cost varies depending on the size and complexity of the project. Start by applying for a building permit from the city. Then, interview contractors. With a building permit and a good contractor, you can build a safe place for a family who wants to rent. You will also reduce your liability. Buyers love basement suites that are registered because the rental income can be used to help them qualify for a bigger mortgage. As such, homes with legal basements sell for more. If a homeowner borrows $100,000 from the principal residence and uses it to build a secondary suite, the annual mortgage payment will be about $5,000, half being principal reduction and the interest portion becomes tax deductible. The basement will generate an annual income of about $20,000. This investment is worth exploring because it is a profitable venture. Seek the assistance of an accountant.

Become a money lender. Amrita borrowed $200,000 from her home at 1.75%. She invested it in second mortgages at 12%, making a yearly profit of $15,400. She called this her vacation money. Always lend in small batches. For example, lend to four different people instead of one. By doing so, you are spreading your risk. Ensure that the loan-to-value ratio does not exceed 85%. Avoid lending on rental properties. Many mortgage brokers can assist in securing second mortgages. Usually, the borrower pays the mortgage broker and solicitor fees. In many cases, they will also pay the investor a finder's fee of about 3-5% of the loan amount. Always choose your own lawyer when investing in a second mortgage.

Study the above ideas carefully and then, prioritize them. Next, get started. In the wise words of Lao Tzu, a journey of a thousand miles begins with a single step.

HOW IT WORKS

Your lender will send out their appraiser and eventually they will require a lawyer to register the secure line. Some lenders may offer this service as a packaged deal. A secure line of credit is like a credit card where the credit limit is high.

For investment purposes, take the maximum allowed. I recommend $100,000 and above. Imagine a credit card with a low interest rate that you can use at any time to buy anything! In this case, you have a vehicle to take you on the path to financial freedom.

Your secure line is money available for your use. If you are planning on moving up to another home, do so and keep your first home as an investment property. Other than that, use the secure line to buy your first investment property. The interest payment on the secure line becomes a tax write-off since you are borrowing the money with the expectation of profiting via investment!

CHECKLIST FOR UTLIZING HOME EQUITY

- ☐ Home Equity Line of Credit arranged
- ☐ Line of credit negotiated for the maximum amount allowed and lowest rate possible
- ☐ Investment alternatives evaluated
- ☐ Following considered:
  - ○ The degree of risk involved
  - ○ The rate of return
  - ○ Best investment selected to maximize Rate of Return.

3.07 BUYING INVESTMENT PROPERTIES

Investing in residential real estate is one of the easiest ways to gain financial freedom. Take the home you are currently living in for instance. Over the years, it probably went up tremendously in value. Investing is like planting seeds. The more seeds planted and cared for will give a bountiful harvest. When buying residential real estate, here are some ideas you can use to enhance your portfolio.

NEGOTIATING

There are many reasons why a seller may want to sell his property. By understanding his motivation, you can negotiate for a better price.

Ask the realtor for a list of similar properties that have sold in the area. This will give you an idea what fair market value is.

Sometimes the seller might have bought another home and needs a specific closing date. Give them the date they want but hold out for your price. Always give something to get something: firm offers, the seller's preferred closing date, extra time to move out of the property, strong deposits, etc.

This is what you can offer to lower the purchase price.

Avoid negotiating tactics that can be perceived as criticizing. For example, don't tell the seller that the home needs painting or the carpet is ugly, and hope for a lower price. This kind of strategy does not work since it puts down the seller, who generally has an emotional connection to the property. You want the seller on your side to get a good deal!

During the process of negotiating a deal for one of my clients, I found out that the seller was taking care of an elderly person who had left his entire estate to the caregiver. The caregiver's aim was to get the home sold quickly and return to her home country.

I submitted an offer $70,000 below market value with two-weeks closing. The seller countered the offer with $30,000 off the list price. I re-countered at the original offer price but removed my buyer's conditions of financing and inspection. I also increased the deposit from $10,000 to $20,000 and added to the offer that $5,000 will be given directly to the seller upon acceptance. The seller accepted the offer. She got $5,000 upfront to buy her airline ticket and the buyer got the home at a discount. That's a win-win strategy.

Try these negotiating ideas:

First, listen. You cannot learn by talking. God gave us two ears and one mouth for a reason.

Repeat what the person said in a question. Then stay silent. For example, you are at a dealership, buying a car and the dealer wants $10,000. You can repeat the amount in a questionable manner, then stay silent. "Ten thousand dollars?" More often they would respond, with a lower price.

In negotiating, the one who has more options, wins. A good negotiator must have many options or the perception of having more options. If the seller has four offers on the table, then he has the advantage. Look for the main reason why the seller wants to sell and that's his hot button!

Once you know the reason the seller wants to sell, keep that as the primary focus. Make it his headache...then sell him the aspirin (the solution).

When the negotiations reach a point where no one wants to bend, work on splitting the difference. I recall a transaction where we were $20,000 apart from closing the deal. I managed to have the buyer and seller split the difference. They were all happy to get it over, knowing that it was a team effort to put it together.

Always trade. For example, a buyer can give the seller the date he needs for a lower price.

At the end, ask for small concessions, such as can you leave the lawn mower, please?

CHECKLIST FOR BUYING INVESTMENT PROPERTIES

- ☐ Location is ideal and meets my criteria
- ☐ Home has potential for growth and "spillover"
- ☐ Preliminary discussions held with Financial Institution for a Line Of Credit
- ☐ Negotiation strategy for the purchase developed with real estate salesperson

3.08 REAL ESTATE BUBBLE

A real estate bubble is when property prices climb rapidly to an unsustainable level and then crash. Sales in many large urban areas in North America have climbed astronomically over the last decade. This trend is expected to continue as demand from immigration and population growth places stress on existing accommodation, which is in limited supply.

With prices continuously climbing, one may wonder when, or even if, prices will come down. The question is, how do we know when the market trend switches from a seller's market to a buyer's market?

It is important to understand the different dynamics in real estate. By keeping an eye out for the right signals, we can better predict the future. Always go against the trend to get the best value for your money. Buy when everyone is selling and sell when everyone is buying.

FROTH

The period leading up to a market crash is known as the froth. Evidence of froth in many urban areas may result in sudden price increases. Here are some indicators:

- Homeowners are renovating and living longer in their homes

- Senior citizens choosing to live in their homes instead of moving to retirement homes

- Fewer homes for sale

- At least two thirds of homes sold are above the original asking price

EVIDENCE OF DANGER IN A BUBBLE

Bubbles can burst when there is an increase in supply to offset the demand. Supply can increase when there are more properties being built than needed. Consider Toronto, known as the crane capital of Canada, where new condos are always sprouting. An interest rate hike may significantly lower demand. With COVID-19, interest rates dropped to a new low. You can arrange a five-year mortgage for around 1.7%. As the city normalizes, interest rates will climb, and the tide can change.

Several jurisdictions in Canada and the U.S impose taxes on the purchase and sale of property if you are a non-resident. Provincial governments, including Ontario and British Columbia, have recently expressed interest in taxing foreign property owners who neither reside nor rent out their properties. [Check with your tax accountant if this applies to you]. Such changes might increase the supply available to Canadians, driving down prices. However, also consider that lower prices can result in higher demand, further complicating the issue.

In 1989, interest rates shot up. Prices plummeted and speculators who were in for a quick profit went bankrupt. In 2007, there was a similar situation in the United States. Prior to both crashes, house prices climbed steeply and then plummeted with unprecedented speed. In 2017, the hot real estate market in the Greater Toronto Area, like in many other big cities, created a bubble which was eventually deflated by government intervention. Sometimes, even the best economists cannot predict when a bubble will burst. The key takeaway is to avoid spreading yourself financially thin.

HOW TO MINIMIZE THE IMPACT OF A FINANCIAL MELTDOWN

Although homes increase in value over time, sometimes it is better to pay down one's remaining mortgage. Lines of credit (such as HELOCs) should be used for investment purposes. Never max out on the credit limit; use only half and keep the other half for emergencies.

Building a basement apartment with money borrowed from the line of credit, for example, is money well spent. Trends are changing and with high housing costs, homes with basement apartments are selling for more. An average basement apartment may cost about $60,000 to build and can fetch almost $20,000 rental income per year. That's an impressive rate of return in which it takes only three years to recapture your investment purely on a cash flow basis (i.e., not including any added value to the house due to renovation or tax payable on the Net Income from rental). From that point, the income less the operating expenses will add to your wealth.

Real estate should be part of a long-term plan and homeowners should use some of the equity in their home to buy investment properties. Avoid the temptation of buying pre-construction properties with the intention of flipping for a profit because a shift in the market can be ruinous. The best investment properties are homes on large lots in mature neighborhoods. The suburbs are still affordable, and, with time, land will appreciate.

There will always be froth in the major urban areas and first-time buyers should buy what they can afford, stepping away from paying rent and moving towards building equity. Invest in a Registered Retirement Savings Plan (RRSPs in Canada) and similar tax-free vehicles and save some tax dollars. Tax-free savings can be used towards a down payment for a property.

Ask yourself what your housing needs will be like in ten years before you decide to move, and then adjust your plan accordingly. Five years ago, a family upgraded from a smaller home into their current home, catering to their adult children.

Eventually, the children moved on and the family now wants to downsize. Big homes require more day-to-day cleaning as well as long-term maintenance, more utilities, and higher taxes, and in a recession, drop much more in value than smaller ones.

If there is a bubble and we are not prepared for it, we can suffer significant financial distress. However, waiting for the bubble to burst can prevent us from building wealth. I saw a poster of an old man and the caption read "This is the young man who is still waiting for real estate prices to come down". No one knows if the bubble will burst but let's be cautious. Use credit to invest and pay cash for luxuries. Don't get caught in the frenzy to buy when prices are escalating and have probably reached their peak.

CHECKLIST FOR AVOIDING IMPACT OF REAL ESTATE BUBBLE:

- ☐ LOC (Line of Credit) used for investment purposes only

- ☐ Half of LOC used, balance retained for flexibility in opportune investments

- ☐ Real Estate Market Metrics developed to:

    - ○ Analyze trends in market swings

    - ○ Determine right time for investment

3.09 ASSIGNMENT SALES

From the time a contract to purchase is signed and possession is given, the buyer's circumstances might have changed, due to, for example, job relocation, financing, or family structure. Originally, Assignment Sales offered a way out where the original buyer can salvage their deposit and a new buyer can close the deal. It has now evolved into a profitable venture.

An Assignment Sale occurs when a buyer (Buyer A) who bought a property, sells the original contract of purchase of sale to a second buyer (Buyer B). By doing so, Buyer A (the assignor) has assigned the original purchase of sale contract to Buyer B (the assignee). The assigned price can be the original purchase price or for a profit or loss. The assignee would then complete the sale with the original seller.

An assignment sale can be for any purchase—resale or newly built. It is most common in new condo sales. With the high demand for housing, some newly built condos double in price before they are ready for occupancy, attracting many speculators. For example, Eric bought a pre-constructed condo for $300,000. During the time lag between purchase and completion, the price increased to $500,000. Eric sold his contract to

Jane for $500,000. He had paid the builder 20% or $60,000 as a down payment. Jane paid Eric $260,000 which represents Eric's down payment and profit. Jane now owes the builder $240,000 and will complete the sale with the builder. Eric more than tripled his deposit money and avoided paying closing costs such as land transfer tax, since that is done only on completing the sale. Most builders allow assignments, subject to approval. Usually, there is an assignment fee imposed by the builder. There may also be other terms in the sales contract which govern assignment. If in doubt, consult a lawyer before proceeding.

An Assignment Sale involves three parties: the seller, the assignor, and the assignee. There are three transactions: the first between the assignor and the seller, the second between the assignor and the assignee, and the third between the assignee and the original seller. Most builders do not allow buyers to advertise assignment sale properties. A buyer caught advertising may be in breach of the sale contract and may find the deal canceled and the deposit forfeited.

With strong demands for housing and endless bidding wars for resale properties, assignment sales are becoming increasingly popular, allowing the buyer to purchase a contract without the bidding frenzy. Assignment Sales are beneficial to both parties. The assignor can sell his unit before it is completed, and the new buyer can save by offering a lesser price compared to the builder's current price. Another hidden advantage is that the lag time is shorter because most assignment sales occur just before occupancy. The new buyer may be able to choose some of the finishes if the unit is not completed by then. In the above example, if Jane cannot complete the sale with the builder, Eric is still obligated. If the market has declined, then Eric would be in trouble, risking his $60,000 and a potential lawsuit from the builder. Assignment sale is a boon in a hot market but a boom in a declining one. It is risky business.

There are tax implications for the assignor and assignee. Jane in our story paid $200,000 for the assignment and a rebate of $60,000 for the deposit. However, if the sale is subject to HST, then it is calculated on the full amount, $260,000. Eric must declare his profit as business income in the year the assignment took place.

Some builders would credit the buyers on HST by adjusting the sale price. If the buyer (Assignor) assigns the property to another buyer (Assignee) and since it is a new property, CRA [Canadian Revenue Authority] considers the assignor as a second builder. The Assignor owes CRA the HST [Harmonized Sales Tax in Canada] rebate for the first purchase. Since the assignor is considered as the second builder, HST is due on the assignment sale as well. In such a case, the HST is added to the assignment sale price and the assignee can apply for HST rebate directly through Revenue Canada. [Check with your tax accountant for liability and treatment of the HST]

When planning an assignment sale, it is best to complete one project at a time. Some try to maximize their profit by purchasing many properties. With the uncertainties and tax implications involved, pursuing multiple properties simultaneously means more room for error.

CHECKLIST FOR ASSIGNMENT SALES

- ☐ Reputable builders found in a good location
- ☐ The builder will allow the buyer to assign the agreement
- ☐ The buyer has declared the builder's fee for any assignment
- ☐ Tax accountant consulted on tax implications for Assignment Sales
- ☐ I have resources to close the transaction if assignment is not possible
- ☐ Closing the transaction will NOT leave me financially exposed

3.10 INVESTING IN LAND

Imagine a product that is in great demand but that cannot be manufactured. Raw land, unlike buildings, does not need to be maintained. Additionally, the property taxes are cheaper, and the owner does not need fire insurance. While an investment in land is potentially lucrative, there are many factors to consider.

LOCATION

Land in a prime location will appreciate faster in value. A plot of land in the downtown core may be worth much more compared to the same size of land in the suburbs. However, while property value is paramount, consider your neighbours. John, an investor, bought a parcel of land next to a gas station. One of the underground tanks of the gas station was leaking and the contaminants had leeched into his land. The clean-up cost was paid for by the owner of the gas station, but it took many years before John could build on the land. When buying land near commercial developments, it is important to get an environmental report before proceeding.

ZONING

Zoning, at its most general level, allows municipalities to assign plots of land to be utilized for different purposes. For example, a factory requires industrial zoning and so cannot be built in the middle of a low-density residential subdivision. The municipality carves out spaces and designates them as commercial, agricultural, residential, industrial and hospitality. Land can be rezoned based on needs and for the greater good of communities. When buying vacant land, it is important to check with the local municipality before committing. I recall an incident where a buyer bought 80 acres of land, hoping to subdivide it. There was a stream running across the property and the city would not allow the developer to build. The buyer sold the land at a loss. Twenty years later, a new buyer had the land rezoned for residential purposes and the property value quadrupled overnight.

PUBLIC UTILITIES

Public utilities such as gas, electricity, water, and a sewer system can make a major impact on the land. Philip bought a motel that sat on five acres of land in Ontario cottage country. The motel had city water and electricity but no gas and no sewer system. A few years later, the town installed a sewer system and a natural gas line. The site was zoned as commercial, and a developer paid three times the acquisition value to build a plaza.

An investor made a conditional offer to purchase a 40-acre plot of land on the outskirts of Barrie, Ontario, subject to due diligence. During her due diligence timeline, she discovered from city hall that it would take over ten years before the municipality could install utilities there. In the process, she learnt that they were planning to install utilities in another part of the city within a few years. She scouted the vacant land in that location and invested there instead.

IMPORTANCE OF A SURVEY

A land survey is a map prepared by a licensed land surveyor that delineates the boundaries of the land, the topography and any buildings on it. To be useful, a survey should be no older than five years.

Nigel bought a seemingly great plot of land on the internet. It was a five-acre parcel about a day's drive away from Toronto. Distance didn't matter to him. He bought the land for recreational sports. Later, Nigel discovered that the five-acre plot only had a frontage of seven feet—something that would have been revealed in a survey.

FINANCING RAW LAND

It is easier to finance a property with a building on it compared to undeveloped land. A building can be rented, creating an income stream, but a parcel of undeveloped land cannot pay the bills. Raw land takes longer to sell and is less appealing to lenders. Land that is close to the city and has all the services and building permits in place is easier to finance. When buying a home, buyers can invest between 5% to 20% and finance the difference. With raw land, the lender may lend to a maximum of 50% of the value. This creates an opportunity for small investors. When buying land, always make the agreement subject to financing, zoning, and satisfactory environmental report.

Buying and selling land can become a profitable venture. Nathan bought a parcel of land for $3,500. He advertised the land for sale at $6,500, offering the buyer to buy with an initial down payment of $1,000 and a monthly mortgage for the balance at 11% for five years. This worked out to be $119 monthly. A series of small investments like this can quickly create an income stream. Nathan managed to generate a monthly cash flow by buying and selling small parcels of land in a business with few competitors.

LAND LOCKED AND FLOOD ZONE PROPERTIES

Road access can be an issue for rural properties. A land-locked property is one that is sandwiched between other properties and the only way to get there is through a neighbor's property. The owner of the land-locked property can try to negotiate a right of way with the owner of the adjacent property for a fee. If that fails, the matter can be taken to the courts to establish a right of way or enforce an easement (if any).

Many properties near large bodies of water are prone to not only flooding but also subsidence. This is becoming even more critical with the impact of Global Warming and its impact on climate change. Before purchasing, do your research. The best place to start is by visiting the local municipal office.

There are countless other factors involved in land investment. Good parcels of land in great neighborhoods are expensive. Sometimes a few partners can pool together and enjoy the rich return on their investment while lowering their individual risk.

CHECKLIST FOR LAND INVESTMENT

- ☐ Land is in a prime location
- ☐ Environmental report obtained if needed
- ☐ Land is not in a flood zone
- ☐ Land is zoned for the right purpose
- ☐ Land can easily be rezoned by application to municipality [confirmed before Offer is made]
- ☐ The land is serviced, or plans exist for installation of services
- ☐ A land survey has been obtained

- ☐   Land is not land-locked but if it is, a right-of-way is possible

- ☐   Financing has been explored and is accessible

- ☐   Offer will be made with conditions

3.11 UNDERSTANDING RENT-TO-OWN

Rent-to-own is a contractual arrangement between the owner and the tenant where in addition to paying the rent, the tenant will put money towards a down payment. Usually, a rental contract will have an option to purchase but this must not be confused with a rent-purchase deal. The first is an option where the tenant is granted the first chance to buy. The second is a purchase where the tenant is legally obligated to buy at the end of the term.

Rent-to-own helps the buyer to own a home in the future and gives the seller an exit strategy. Rent-to-own attracts investors who enjoy the profits from real estate without the hassle from tenants. Usually, the closing date is set between three to five years into the future. Tenants who enter the rent-to-own program can gradually save their down payment or improve their credit score, knowing that they will eventually own the home. In such cases, a tenant is being paired with an investor. The tenant can shop for the property of their choice. The investor will make the initial purchase and then the investor and the tenant can enter a rent-to-own contract.

ASPECTS OF A RENT-TO-OWN PROGRAM

To enter the program, the tenant usually pays an option fee of around 2.5% of the purchase price. If the tenant cannot close the transaction at the end of the term, then the option fee is forfeited by the seller. In addition to the negotiated rent, the tenant pays an additional monthly amount that would be credited towards the down payment on closing. Usually, the purchase price is set up front.

In a rising market, prices can climb substantially above the set price. The difference between the set price and the current value can augment the tenant's down payment.

STEPS IN A RENT-TO-OWN PROGRAM

1. Engage a lawyer in the process.
2. Conduct an inspection. Usually, the tenant is responsible for all repairs, including appliances, and improvements. If the home requires work, then it might not be worth the effort. In some cases, the tenant can complete renovations for a discounted price.
3. Register the rent-purchase deal.

Since this arrangement helps the tenant to transition from being a tenant to becoming a homeowner by allowing the tenant to gradually save up enough for a down payment and in many cases improve their credit, it's a win-win for both parties. Sellers benefit as well because they enjoy a positive cash flow without the worry about maintenance, repairs, or tenant problems. Both parties' interests are aligned. Over the years, the seller would have paid down their mortgage and will have built some equity in the home.

In a rent-to-own program, a seller is obligated to sell the home to the tenant, but the tenant is not contractually obligated to purchase. However, if the tenant does not exercise the option to purchase, the tenant loses his down payment. A tenant who is unable to arrange financing at the end of the term can suffer if the landlord enforces his right to obtain the forfeited down payment and then sells the property to another buyer.

The intention in a rent-to-own option is for both parties to mutually benefit. It is highly advisable to engage a lawyer and understand what is in the contract before committing.

DUE DILIGENCE

Like all real estate purchases, both parties should be diligent in their approach. It is best to engage a solicitor who is familiar with rent-to-own.

Other provisions, the contract must include:

- Purchase price
- Original deposit
- Closing date
- Amount of rent
- Additional deposits and
- Who will maintain the property?

In rent-to-own, the usual landlord and tenant rules apply. For example, if there is no heat in the home, it is the landlord's responsibility to address.

Rent-to-own is a viable proposition in a hot real estate market. Investors benefit because a rent-to-own tenant will take care of the investment, knowing that they will eventually become the owner. Investors receive an upfront deposit, a higher than market value sale, and secure rent. The tenant enjoys a home where they can raise a family knowing that sometime in the future, they will become the proud owner. When greed is taken out of the recipe, it's a win-win.

CHECKLIST FOR RENT-TO-OWN

- ☐ Lawyer familiar with the process retained
- ☐ House inspection completed
- ☐ Property assessed for fair market value
- ☐ Contract contains all essential clauses including:
  - ○ Purchase price
  - ○ Deposit
  - ○ Closing date
  - ○ Amount of rent
  - ○ Responsibility for property maintenance
- ☐ Rent-purchase agreement registered on property title
- ☐ Confirmation of financing will be available for tenant once down payment is made

3.12 INVESTING IN SECOND MORTGAGES

Second mortgages can be both a safe and lucrative investment, but only if done correctly. A second mortgage is a loan that is registered on the title of a property. It is called either a "second mortgage" or a "junior mortgage" because the first mortgage is senior, and in the event of default, the first mortgagee gets paid first and then the second. Second mortgages have higher rewards but are exposed to higher risks.

Reasons why people might need a second mortgage include:

> 1. With the new "Stress Test" (applies to Canada; check in your own jurisdiction for applicability), buyers will qualify for smaller mortgages and to make up the shortfall, they will resort to borrowing private funds
>
> 2. Others may need it because of their poor credit rating, or being self-employed or to start a new business
>
> 3. Securing a loan for investment purposes by offering equity in the house as collateral

Jacob and Andrea receive a $2,000 cash flow every month from their home. They took a home equity line of credit for $300,000 at 4% against their home and loaned it as a second mortgage at 13.75%. In addition to the high interest rate, the lender can charge finder fees.

The lender would give the borrower a lump sum amount and in return the borrower would make regular monthly payments by electronic withdrawal or post-dated cheques to the lender.

WHEN INVESTING IN SECOND MORTGAGES

1.   Always assess your risk when lending. The first and second mortgages should not exceed 85% of the value of the property. If the borrower defaults, there is enough equity in the property to cover.

2.   Lend only on the borrower's principal residence and avoid lending to "investors". Investors who accept loans above 10% are usually spread thin and in the event of a price drop, the equity will be depleted, putting the collateral at risk.

3.   If lending to investors, ask for a blanket second mortgage where the mortgage amount is registered on multiple properties. With a blanket mortgage, the lender can have more security because the mortgage is on many homes.

4.   Before lending, make sure the home is marketable. It is better to lend on a home in Toronto or a major urban area than one in Thunder Bay or a remote area where demand is much lower. The equity secured in the

property will be worthless if there are no potential buyers.

5. For similar reasons, avoid lending to owners with large expensive homes. Large expensive homes take longer to sell, and chances are the first mortgage and property taxes will be substantial. The amount of the second mortgage should be between $25,000 and $50,000 to reduce risk. If you have $100,000 to invest, then invest in three second-mortgages.

STEPS IN INVESTING IN SECOND MORTGAGES

1. Let the borrower complete a mortgage application

2. Find out the reasons the borrower needs the money

3. Get a credit search done and review the application along with the credit report

4. Ask for a job letter, recent pay stubs and T4 slips for the past 2 years

5. If the borrower is self-employed, ask for the last two years of tax returns. This is to make sure that they are paying their taxes because, in the event of a default, taxes will take precedence over any mortgages

6. Use a lawyer to complete the transaction. Your lawyer will prepare the necessary documents, and oversee signing

7. The money is given to your lawyer in trust. In many instances, there are two lawyers involved—the borrower's lawyer and the lender's lawyer

8. All the costs involved, including your lawyer's fees, are paid by the borrower (unless otherwise negotiated)

9. The term of the mortgage is usually for one year and can be extended if both parties agree

10. Always use your own lawyer and not the borrower's lawyer. Typically, the borrower will pay your lawyer's legal costs to secure the second mortgage

You can find second mortgages by placing ads or by contacting lawyers, mortgage brokers and realtors. Many mortgage brokers will help for a fee, called a brokerage fee, which the borrower pays.

Second mortgage holders sometimes sell their portfolios for a discount. For example, a $40,000 mortgage at 13% can be sold for $35,000 at 13% because the mortgagee wants to cash out. Calculate the cost/benefit of this before proceeding.

Many investors choose second mortgages because of low administrative costs, and it functions as a passive source of income. Money depreciates on a long-term basis and one of the best strategies is to invest in real estate in the early years to build equity and then use that equity to lend second mortgages.

CHECKLIST FOR SECOND MORTGAGES:

☐ Application for the mortgage completed

☐ Total mortgage amount does not exceed 85% of the property value

☐ Mortgage is on the principal residence

☐ Investment is spread around several properties

☐ Term of the mortgage should be about one year

☐ Credit report obtained from the borrower

☐ Tax returns of borrowers evaluated for accuracy of the application

☐ Lawyer engaged for the transaction [All transactions should be reviewed and endorsed by your lawyer]

3.13. RRSP MORTGAGES

Saving for retirement in a tax-deductible registered savings plan account (in Canada a Registered Retirement Savings Plan or RRSP) is one of the few tax benefits remaining for taxpayers. With this strategy, you can free up your RRSP and use it to invest without breaking it. Most contributors do not manage their investment portfolios and rely on their financial institutions to do the job. Their savings are invested in mutual funds, often subject to high management fees. The high fees reduce the profit and slow the growth of their investments.

Another strategy is to invest in a registered mortgage plan where the investor has more control. A RRSP mortgage is like a bank mortgage where the bank lends the money and holds the property as security. In this situation, the investor holds the mortgage on a specific property. This is called a private mortgage and the terms and conditions are negotiated by both the lender and the borrower. Since it is a private mortgage, investors must do their own due diligence.

Investors must find a financial institution that allows RRSP mortgages. Most financial institutions prefer to give a mortgage directly to a buyer rather than invest their clients RRSP. With a RRSP mortgage, the banks are losing profit from both sides. A few financial institutions such as Canadian Western Trust, Olympia Trust and TD Waterhouse offer RRSP Mortgages for a fee.

SETTING UP A RRSP MORTGAGE

Open a self-directed RRSP with the company and transfer all the existing RRSP into it. This may take some time because the RRSP holder must liquidate the current portfolios and pool the money into one account. There are no tax penalties because the investor is simply transferring funds from one registered account to another.

Financial institutions will act as a trustee for the RRSP mortgage. The process of qualifying is the same as if the borrower is applying for a mortgage where income verification, credit search and approval are required.

To set up a RRSP mortgage, the costs involved are:

- Administrative costs

- CMHC fees and appraisal fees

- The original set-up fees (can be a few thousand dollars)

- Monitoring costs a few hundred dollars every year

HOW IT OPERATES

Once the RRSP mortgage is set up, it operates just like a regular mortgage where the borrower makes regular monthly payments to the investor's RRSP. The cash accumulated can be reinvested. If there is a default, the trustee is responsible for selling the property under power of sale.

With RRSP mortgages, the interest rate is the posted rate under which the mortgage has been taken out and not the discounted rate. As such, you will be receiving a higher interest on your mortgage payment and a higher interest income will be going to the RRSP.

However, let's assume that you borrow from your RRSP at 4% and your rate of return is 6%. This means the spread is only 2%. If you borrow from the banks at a discounted rate of 3% and invest at 6%, then the spread or profit will be greater.

It is not a vehicle to use for principal residence, but a RRSP mortgage can be beneficial when purchasing a rental property. The higher interest paid to the RRSP is a tax-deductible expense against personal income and higher interest earnings for the RRSP holder.

Most RRSP mortgages are second mortgages with returns between 12% to 14% plus finder's fees and lawyer fees.

THINGS TO WATCH FOR

As a private lender, the investor must ensure that the investment is sound. It is important that the borrower has about 15% of their own money invested in the property. This is called a loan-to-value ratio or LTV. The higher the LTV, the greater the risk for the borrower and greater the chance of default.

For novice investors, seek expert advice from a mortgage broker, real estate broker and a lawyer. Investors can free up their RRSP by giving themselves a RRSP mortgage on their principal residence and releasing some equity to invest. Having an RRSP mortgage is an innovative strategy where investors have full control of their investment portfolios and can avoid high mutual fund fees. With RRSP mortgages, the portfolio should be substantial—at least $50,000 and above will work.

CHECKLIST FOR RRSP MORTGAGES

- ☐ All set-up costs have been considered:
  - o Admin costs
  - o CMHC fees [in Canada, Central Mortgage and Housing Corp]
  - o Appraisal fees/ monitoring cost annually
- ☐ The borrower has invested at least 15% of his or her own money

☐   The RRSP mortgage has a higher net return than obtainable from a conventional RRSP

☐   All angles are explored and explained by professionals like a mortgage broker, real estate broker and a lawyer

3.14 TEAMWORK

Pooling your money with others for investment purposes can give you the strength and courage you need to start your investment portfolio. However, there can be both benefits and drawbacks with this decision.

You share both the risks and the rewards. With more money, a higher income level and great teammates, you can create more wealth since your investment pool increases.

Just like a marriage, you must choose your partner carefully. Your partner should bring his or her own strengths and skills to the relationship. Getting into a relationship might be sweet but getting out can be bitter! Always have an exit strategy drawn up with a buy-out clause included, even if you don't think you will need it. Always look for someone you can trust and work with.

HOW TO PROCEED

1. Prepare a Partnership Agreement based on a mutual understanding. If it is a short-term arrangement, then consider a joint venture arrangement. A joint venture is when two or more parties agree to work together on

a specific project. For example, a contractor who provides the labour and expertise in doing renovations and an investor who finances such projects.

2.   The terms of the joint venture are spelt out and apply only to that project. For instance, in a renovation project, the investor can provide necessary capital while the contractor can provide labor. In this case, each party is responsible for their own accounting.

3.   If it is for a long-term arrangement, then consider establishing a partnership agreement or a corporation. Partnership agreements are when two or more parties have a formal arrangement to operate a business. There are tax advantages in establishing a partnership, but each partner is on the hook for any liabilities caused by the other partner.

4.   When it comes to exposure for liabilities of a business entity, corporations are safer since the personal assets of the shareholder are protected. An owner can have shares in the corporation and is not liable for the day-to-day operation. (However, corporations are double taxed, first on the profits and then the shareholders will pay taxes based on the dividends received, depending on the jurisdiction and the type of corporation). [Check with your Tax Accountant]

Partnerships are great for projects like buying and holding land on a long term. Prime land is expensive. The best way is to have many investors pooling their money and purchasing prime land. These projects do not require day-to-day care and as such makes great long-term projects. Projects that involve day to day operation can create more friction between investors and eventually become less sustainable.

CHECKLIST FOR TEAMWORK

☐ Partnership agreement drawn up by a competent, independent professional. (Avoid having the agreement drafted by someone who a mediator—or judge, would consider biased and involved in a conflict of interest).

☐ Aims and objectives of the partnership have been defined

☐ Exit strategy has been built into the agreement, including terms of dissolution or withdrawal of the principals

☐ Separation of responsibilities and functions are enshrined in the agreement

☐ Criteria for profit/loss sharing is clearly defined in the agreement

3.15 BUILDING WEALTH

Investment is a slow but steady process. Many people are scared to venture into real estate investment. *Fear is paralyzing.* It is *false evidence appearing real.* The more we harbor it, the greater it becomes. The law of attraction takes over and we only attract the negative but if we guard our thoughts and embrace our fears rationally, armed with facts and figures, watch them disappear.

In real estate, I've come across people who analyze everything and by the time they finish, someone else has already snapped up the investment. As the saying goes, *if you are sure-footed in the world of real estate, then you will never leave the shore.*

A negative cash flow can drain you. A positive cash flow is essential to compounding your wealth. The word currency comes from "current" which means flow. If you have many small positive cash flows, your passive income stream will become torrential. Avoid buying properties with negative cash flow. They dry up your income stream and force you to become a distressed seller. This does not mean that properties with negative cash flow are bad investments. I love to buy commercial properties with negative cash flow because I can get them at a discounted price. With time, there is room to increase the rent. Properties with high rent might be great for cash flow but because the rent is already high, it's difficult to increase it. It is easier to lose your tenants with other competing rental spaces when the rent is high.

TREATING YOUR INVESTMENT AS A BUSINESS

1.   Set up a separate account and don't use rental income for anything other than property related expenses.

2.   Maintain the property and you will attract good tenants. A run-down property will attract the wrong tenant.

3.   Invest in small rental properties in the early stages where it is easier to generate a positive cash flow.

4.   Don't be in a great hurry to build your portfolio. Exercising patience will bring worthwhile results. Impatience and emotion should be taken out of the equation.

5.   Good deals exist when problems are encountered. For example, if the home is tenanted and the owner wants to get out, you can often buy at a discounted price.

6.   Renovating a home will increase its value and a newly renovated property will attract good, high-paying tenants.

RECESSION-PROOF YOUR INVESTMENTS

In a recession, the rental market is better. Prepare by doing the following:

- Have fixed long-term mortgages on your properties

- Always prepare for an emergency

- Every year, increase the rent according to the rental guidelines. Take advantage of that because if you don't, then later, you will have underperforming assets

- When one of your rental properties becomes vacant, modernize it and increase the rent to fair market value

SOME PRECAUTIONS

1. Many investors are of the opinion that it does not matter which lender they borrow money from. It is important to shop around. Interest rate varies from one lender to the next.

2. It is necessary to review the commitment letter and the mortgage statement from the lender you are considering. Some lenders may charge less interest but impose hefty lenders' fees, while others may charge for a simple mortgage renewal.

3. Avoid second, third and blanket mortgages. A second and third mortgage will result in higher interest rate payments while a

blanket mortgage allows the lender to tie up your other investments as security for their loan.

4.   Each property should have its mortgage from a reputable lender. If the interest rate is low, lock in for a long term and if it is high, then go with a shorter term.

5.   Let your bank be your police against bad investments. I invested in a commercial property and the bank refused to finance it because of the low income declared. My business partner and I decided to pay cash. Later, when we decided to sell, the buyer had a difficult time arranging a mortgage as well. Had we followed the lender's advice in the first place, we could have avoided that purchase. Paying cash was a bad idea as well because that money would have been a sizable down payment on a better performing asset such as a retail plaza.

Real estate values usually double every seven to ten years. Therefore, the equity built up during those years can be used to invest in another property. Four residential properties at retirement, each earning two thousand, five hundred dollars monthly gives you an annual income stream of $120,000. That beats the average RRSP.

CHECKLIST FOR BUILDING WEALTH

☐ Criteria of business essentials established

☐ Recession-proof measures in place

☐ Precautionary measures launched

☐ ROI (return on investment) evaluation understood and in place

☐ System of warning signs for over-exposure established

☐ Net Worth analysis feature in evaluating my exposure to debt

☐ Pros and cons of a partnership evaluated before signing on

3.16 SELLING A HOUSE TO MAXIMIZE PROFIT

On your path to financial freedom and eventually retirement, you might decide to sell properties. You might do this to rid yourself of troublesome assets or buy a larger house to live in. Both scenarios raise the question: if you must, when is the best time to sell?

Although there's no ironclad pattern, the housing market often follows certain yearly trends. The market picks up by mid-January because there are fewer homes for sale and the trend continues into the spring with more buyers and sellers entering the marketplace. The market slows down in the summer months and then picks up in the fall but not to the same extent as the spring. The best time to sell a home is therefore from mid-January to mid-February because of the lack of supply. The media then fans the flames of the hot housing market and buyers, speculators and investors become a feeding frenzy, bidding on everything.

PREPARING THE HOUSE:

1.   Declutter the home to its bare minimum to create space.

2.   Store excess furniture and other items in the garage or off-site.

3.   Hire a professional stager. A home that is well maintained and professionally staged will sell faster and for more money.

Selling is all psychology—sellers must tap into a buyer's emotions. Enough positive responses create an emotional reaction while a few negative responses create a logical decision. People buy emotionally and then justify the purchase with logic. Getting the best price requires triggering a positive emotional response. The art of selling is subliminal, arousing emotions from buyers through their senses: sight, smell, hearing and taste.

Perception is a reality when selling a home. Photography is essential in today's fast paced world. Buyers shop online and narrow their picks. Drone technology, 3-D virtual tours, professional home videos and high-end feature sheets are the new trends.

SELECTING A REALTOR:

1.   Select a realtor based on knowledge, experience and track record instead of relationship alone.

2.   Interview three realtors.

3.   Ask each realtor to prepare a market evaluation of the home and to explain their marketing plan.

4. Look at the realtor's client reviews and how they are currently marketing properties online. The way the realtor markets the home to potential buyers is crucial. Words have power and a realtor's ability to write attractive ads for your home is imperative.

Many sellers opt for a realtor who offers to sell their home at the highest price. This can be a fatal mistake because the realtor does not set the price—the market does. Setting the price is dictated by what similar homes are selling for in your area. Most buyers shop by comparison and would buy the home that stands out in looks and price. The best pricing strategy: price the property slightly less than the competition in the area which may cause more showings and multiple offers.

ON THE MARKET:

1. Allow adequate time between offers.

2. Expose the property for at least a week but have a set offer presentation date.

3. Let the buyers and their representatives meet in person at the home to review offers. The fear of loss is greatest when a buyer sits in anticipation waiting for all the other buyers to give their bids.

In an off-season market, the seller can choose their terms such as closing date, price, and deposit. In many instances, sellers can negotiate a quick closing date and rent back the property until they are ready to move. This is advantageous to the seller because if the price drops, they are protected. Some buyers may choose to walk away from their deposits. Litigation is expensive and time-consuming as well. If the closing date exceeds three months, it is a good idea to ask for a significant upfront deposit. A strong deposit is between five to ten percent of the purchase price. Buyers will think twice about forfeiting such a deposit if things get sour at closing.

Selling your home can be a pleasant experience. Polish your gem of a house and sell when everyone wants to buy. Choose the right realtor and create a working plan. Every dollar counts.

CHECKLIST FOR SELLING

- ☐ All options considered before selling
- ☐ House decluttered and excess furniture stored
- ☐ House cleaned and prepared for sale
- ☐ Criteria established for a realtor
- ☐ Realtor selected based on experience and track record and other criteria
- ☐ Stager and professional photographer engaged
- ☐ House priced slightly below market
- ☐ Offer presentation date set
- ☐ Valuables and important documents secured
- ☐ Plan in place for family to be off-site during showings

SECTION IV: RENTALS

4.01 RENTAL ESSENTIALS

Two weeks prior to moving in, contact your tenants to ensure that they have arranged to transfer all utilities. Request and organize e-transfers for the monthly rent.

Prepare a welcome basket for your new tenants. First impressions are important, and this gesture goes a long way in building relationships and keeping good tenants. A kind gesture can be the start of an extraordinary relationship.

Change the locks for new tenants. The previous occupant may still have a set of the old keys. If there is a garage door opener, change the code.

Meet the tenant on move-in day and give them a walkthrough of the home if you haven't already done so. Have a checklist prepared and go over it with them

WORTHWHILE PRACTICES

Your investment property is an asset because wealth is now flowing towards you. In other words, you are now on the highway to building wealth!

With investment properties, aim to increase the monthly payment to the lenders. By paying down the mortgage faster on the rental property, you build equity at a faster pace. In a few years, you can renegotiate with the lenders and start working towards your next rental property.

Like a fruit tree, just plant the seed, water and nurture the seedling and in time you will enjoy the fruits of your labour.

ALWAYS BUILD UP A RENT RESERVE

Always keep a reserve of about six months of rental payments for property tax and mortgage. After the first six months of rental income, reduce the reserve to four months' worth. Later, arrange for a Secure Line of Credit on the rental property and use that instead, allowing your own money to get back to work. A good reserve is needed for emergencies such as unpaid rent, bad debts from a tenant or unanticipated repairs needed. This reserve is strictly used as a backup.

PROPERTY MANAGEMENT COMPANY

Some investors do not like the hassle involved in renting. There are many management companies that manage investment properties for a fixed percentage of the rent. This does not include the cost of repair. While the fees paid are deductible expenses from the rental income, it could be a drain on your investment.

Over the years I've developed a relationship with contractors who can inspect my rental properties once a year and complete the necessary repairs. A property well cared for will always attract model tenants.

RECORD-KEEPING ON RENTAL PROPERTY

An investor, in the eyes of the government, is conducting a business and so must keep proper records. These records must be supported by original receipts. Some benefits to proper record keeping include:

- Gives an overview of your real estate portfolio

- Shows where you can generate more income

- Provides details on which expenses you can reduce

- Gives you an idea of the past and present financial situation

- Allows you to make better financial plans

- Protects you in the event you are audited

- Borrowing money from financial institutions to invest becomes easier because you can provide the information they may need instantly

Proper record keeping must have four key elements:

- What you did

- Why you did it

- When you did it

- Supporting documents

For example, let's look at re-doing the driveway on a rental property. Keep some form of record, like a photo of the old driveway, record the date the driveway is being re-done and save the invoice along with a track record of your payment. It is a good practice to document and file everything once the task is finished. To start, a simple binder may prove very helpful.

The following Tax implications on rental income and expenditure incurred for rental property should be kept in mind:

1.   Tax treatment can vary from jurisdiction to jurisdiction.

2.   Records should be kept for EACH property.

3.   There should be a clear distinction between expenses of a personal nature and those incurred for the rental property.

4.   Ongoing routine expenses (such as maintenance) can be written off against Rental Income in the year incurred while Capital Expenditure (such as significant improvements to the property) is spread over the life of the project.

As your business grows, you may need to hire a bookkeeper. In any event, hire a competent and accomplished accountant to provide advice and prepare your tax returns.

STAYING IN TOUCH WITH YOUR TENANTS

Purchase six filters for the furnace and drop it off at your rental property. Ask your tenant to replace the filter in the furnace every two months. It cleans the air, protects the furnace and reduces the utility bills.

Every fall, visit the property and replace all batteries in the smoke detectors. Every three years, replace all battery-operated smoke and carbon monoxide detectors. During the Christmas season, visit your tenants and drop off a gift basket. Every year, prior to renewing the lease, conduct an inspection of the property.

CHECKLIST FOR RENTING

☐ Plan in place to create a pleasant environment for tenants

☐ Plan in place to stay in touch with tenants

☐ Reserve fund started for emergencies

☐ Financial Plan drawn up to reduce mortgage and liability faster (to increase equity)

☐ Property Management company hired if needed

☐ Various options for property insurance investigated (stick with the same insurer, if possible, for investment and personal needs)

☐ System in place for accurate and timely record keeping

Competent and experienced bookkeeper/accountant hired to prepare tax returns

4.02 CONVERTING RESIDENCES

If you are planning on upgrading to a larger home, it might be a good idea to convert your current residence into a rental property.

The best way to do so is to first test the waters by placing a few ads on the internet and in the local newspapers to gauge the rental demand in your neighborhood. If you find that the response is low, then adjust your price down and if it is high, adjust up. At this point you can let potential tenants know that you are looking for a good tenant to move into your home in about three to four months.

Approach your lender. The lender will be able to tell you if you are qualified for a second property. If approved, you can increase the mortgage on the current property to the maximum limit and make a larger down-payment on the second property. The interest portion of the mortgage on the rental property is tax deductible against the rental income.

Converting from a principal residence to a rental will have some tax implications. As your principal residence, you are exempted from capital gains tax in Canada — (check with a CPA in your jurisdiction), but since you are converting, you will be exempted from the capital gains tax to this point.

Obtain two to three letters of opinion from realtors about the market value of the home. Alternatively, have it appraised by a home appraiser. Let your accountant know your intention to convert.

CHECKLIST FOR CONVERSIONS

- ☐ Potential for renting the principal residence evaluated

- ☐ Financing for the second property arranged

- ☐ Market value appraisal completed for current property

- ☐ Tax and financial implications discussed with real estate salesperson and CPA

4.03 BASEMENT APARTMENTS

Buyers pay a premium for homes with registered basement apartments because of the immediate income boost they provide. Costs to retrofit and register existing basement apartments vary depending on the municipality, size and amount of labour required. Newly built basement apartments can cost as much as $50,000 and most buyers don't have that kind of cash on hand. Buyers prefer to pay a higher price for a home with a registered basement apartment and include the added cost in their mortgage.

DOWNSIDE OF ILLEGAL BASEMENT APARTMENTS

Chris loved student rentals because they can be profitable.

One snowy morning, a tenant slipped and fell on the driveway. An ambulance was called. The tenant complained that he was experiencing severe head and back pain. He sued Chris for $600,000. Chris' insurance company denied the claim since he had failed to inform them that the house was a rental property. The tenant settled for $500,000.

Chris could have avoided the lawsuit if:

1. He had obtained a municipal zoning change converting the property to a rooming house
2. The insurance company had been informed that the property was a rental
3. He had insisted and verified that the tenant obtain his own insurance
4. The Lease Agreement had stipulated that the tenant was responsible for snow and ice removal

Sometimes we are so caught up in getting the maximum rent from a property that we leave ourselves vulnerable. When we have created Wealth, it's important to protect it.

LEGAL BASEMENT APARTMENTS

1. Registered basement apartments can help buyers qualify for higher mortgages. For example, rent of $1,300 per month can help buyers qualify for an extra $300,000 mortgage at 1.8%. Over 25 years, the amount of total rent collected would be around $230,000. If we use this money to further pay down the mortgage, we can grow our wealth quicker.

2. There are many tax advantages. Rent is considered income and owners can claim expenses in earning that income, such as:

- Proportionate share of utilities and mortgage interest based typically on tenant occupancy

- Share of property insurance

- Cost for repairs and maintenance of rental suites. (Open a separate account, keep proper records, and consult your accountant)

3.　　If the rental property generates a net loss, that loss can be carried forward and written off against future net profit from that property. [Check with your CPA for applicability in your jurisdiction]

4.　　Registered basement apartments may already have good tenants, saving you both time and the cost of attracting new ones. In many jurisdictions, registered basement apartments add to the already low rental housing stock and are much safer than apartment buildings with multiple stories, tenants and elevators as they are accessible from the ground level.

5.　　With population growth and high immigration levels, the demand for rental units continues to increase, and with escalating home prices, registered apartments are becoming trendy.

6.　　Liabilities are reduced once apartments are registered because rental units must pass all final inspections, and homeowners must provide proof of insurance to the municipality. Many homeowners with unregistered apartments fail to inform their insurance providers and that can void their policy.

7.   These secondary suites also provide companionship and assistance for some owners. An elderly couple, for example, may choose a tenant who can assist in lawn care and snow removal for a reduced rent.

RETROFITTING A BASEMENT APARTMENT

In Ontario, there are currently over 230,000 basement apartments! However, most of these are not up to current building codes. Many owners are unaware of the risks involved when renting their basements.

Tenants, neighbours or anyone concerned can report illegal basement apartments to their municipality. Once reported, enforcement officers will step in, and the homeowners must retrofit or reconvert the basement back to a single-family dwelling or face fines ranging from $25,000 to $50,000 depending on the jurisdiction.

Tenants can apply for rent reductions if apartments do not meet health and safety standards. In the event of an accident such as a fire, a flood or a slip and fall, landlords will not be exempted from liability and can be sued.

I do not recommend renting unregistered basement apartments since they can pose a greater risk for owners and tenants who may find themselves facing fines or even added as defendants in a multi-year long personal injury lawsuit.

For example, I recall an incident where a tenant had slipped and fallen and then sued the landlord. The insurance company voided the landlord's insurance policy because the apartment was not up to code and the landlord had not informed the insurance company that the basement was being rented. The landlord paid over half a million dollars out of pocket as settlement, along with the bill for both lawyers.

Once registered, basement apartments attract good tenants because they are safe to rent. Registered basement apartments do not impinge negatively on communities and do not create an overload on services such as sewer and garbage. Most families living in basement apartments are small. Some municipalities offer incentives such as a refund on building permits, increased garbage allowances and two mailboxes to accommodate homeowners. Forgivable grants up to $25,000 are available from time to time for low- or medium-income homeowners to renovate and register their basement apartments. The intention is to create affordable, safe and sustainable rental units.

Registered basement apartments are re-inspected every three years or upon change of ownership [depending on jurisdiction]. The registration can be revoked if homeowners fail to maintain the required standards and keep the rental up to code.

Registered apartments provide extra income for homeowners, safety for tenants, and are a cost-effective way to provide affordable accommodation. It's an income booster for buyers and a price-booster for sellers.

REQUIREMENTS: RETROFITTED BASEMENT APARTMENTS

1.   Before any construction work begins, a building permit is needed from the local municipality. All the construction and labour work must be done by certified trade persons. A city inspector will inspect the job at different stages of construction. After construction, the city's fire, gas and electrical company will conduct a final inspection before you are permitted to rent the space.

2.   To retrofit the suite, the owner will be required to complete an Application for Registration along with a non-refundable filing fee, a survey and a site plan of the home that shows existing structures, driveways and boundaries of the property. The owner must provide a current and a proposed floor plan stamped by an engineer or architect licensed in their jurisdiction. In some jurisdictions the code requires that there must be only one apartment in the basement. The rental suite must be smaller than the main dwelling.

3.   The most important criterion is fire safety. The law requires that the unit be self-contained. In the event of a fire and if the main exit cannot be used, the occupants must have a safe and easily accessible second option

such as a large window they can climb out of, or a second door as an exit.

4.   To reduce smoke inhalation, the unit must have a fire rated self-locking entrance door that is 1.75-inch solid wood or metal and a self- closing mechanism. The ceiling between the upper level and the apartment must have a fire separation such as fire rated drywall and insulation so that fire cannot penetrate easily from one level to the next.

5.   Interconnected smoke alarms, with flashing lights, and carbon monoxide detectors should be installed within each unit and all shared areas.

6.   The furnace room requires fire rated drywall and a fire sprinkler system.

7.   The bathroom and the kitchen fans need to be vented separately to the outside.

8.   All basement apartments need to meet the local building code standards to be approved.

SHOULD AN INVESTMENT PROPERTY HAVE A SECONDARY SUITE?

Investment properties with registered basement apartments will generate more income for the investor. However, there are drawbacks to consider. Many triple A tenants do not want to live in shared accommodations. Landlords may lose out on attracting and keeping these tenants.

With two families, the landlord may have issues such as parking which should be carefully considered. With one family, the landlord can transfer all the utilities in the tenant's name.

Basement apartments can present disturbances for the other tenant. For example, one might be relaxing while the other tenant has a few friends over for a party. Always remember that safety and caring for others comes first, money second!

CHECKLIST FOR BASEMENT APARTMENTS

- ☐ Architectural plan obtained
- ☐ Survey of property completed
- ☐ Application made for registration with municipality
- ☐ Contract signed with experienced builder(s)
- ☐ Completed basement apartment meets all safety and municipal guidelines and is up to code
- ☐ Basement apartment passes inspection by the municipality
- ☐ Certificate issued by municipality

4.04 CHOOSING AWESOME TENANTS

David drank the last bit of coffee as he signed the rental agreement with his new tenant. The previous tenant was self-employed and operated from home as a baker. The entire home had been damaged with mold. Another self-employed tenant had a sewing business, and the furnace was clogged with dust.

A home needs rest, just like an individual. Someone who works as a Health Care professional, for example, will spend less time at home and the home will remain in better shape.

ESSENTIALS: RENTING

1.   Credit is **not** the most important criteria when choosing a good tenant — the source of income is. The perfect tenant with a clean credit and a stable job is ideal. However, over the years I have come to realize that in a matter of time, they will move on. Bruised credit and a stable job may provide you with a long-term, model tenant. A perfect tenant with clean credit and a stable job will be moving on once they can buy their own home.

2.   Ask the tenant to provide a job letter, two recent pay stubs and their tax slips (T4 slips in Canada) for the last two years. I had a reference call once from a landlord who had

rented his home to a reverend but was now faced with a bounced cheque for the first payment! The real story: the reverend was not really a reverend. He had bought his certificate online.

3.   Job stability is important in choosing good tenants. Steady, consistent, long-term employment means a tenant will pay when the rent is due and it's possible to collect unpaid rent through the courts via garnishment as a last resort. Be careful when it comes to self-employed tenants. Wages cannot be garnished from tenants who own their own company as they control when and how much the company pays them personally. Sometimes tenants are "professionals" and know how to outsmart landlords, especially inexperienced ones.

4.   Every tenant must complete a Rental Application and provide a Credit Report which is essential in assessing spending habits. Always check the prospective tenant's debt-to-income ratio. If the prospective tenant's debt ratio is too high, chances are strong that they will default. A good rule of thumb is that their monthly debt payment and rent should not exceed 60% of their net income.

5.   Always meet prospective tenants in person. Ask the entire family to meet and complete the rental application. This will give you time to assess the potential tenants. Never make your decision based on race, gender, religion, disability, family status or any other protected class or grounds in your jurisdiction.

[Some of these assessment criteria might also violate the Human Rights Act in some jurisdictions—check this out with a legal professional if in doubt]

6.   Regarding references, check with the last two landlords and employer. Ask about their cleanliness and if they usually pay rent on time. Inquire as to their social behaviors, such as smoking and late-night parties. Query the way they parted — was it under good or bad terms? **Keep in mind: if a landlord wants to get rid of a bad tenant, the landlord can lie to you as well.**

7.   It is a good practice to visit the client's current place of residence. You can see first-hand how they are living. Do not discount social media. Finding good tenants is more of an art than a science. It is better to seek the help of a professional.

8.   Look for valuable clues to be able to assess a tenant's suitability. Ask a simple question: How many will be living in the property? The next step is to meet all of them, including the children, at the rental property where you can assess the bonding between the parents and the children.

Like a good detective, look beyond the obvious. Consider the car they are driving — is it clean inside? If its dirty, chances are that's the way they will keep the property. Always trust your intuition.

ESSENTIALS: ATTRACTING GOOD TENANTS:

1.   To attract the right tenant, it is important to provide a spotless home. A home that is recently painted and updated with new appliances will attract good tenants while a home with compromising issues such as old, dirty appliances, worn carpet and dusty light fixtures will attract compromising tenants.

2.   Consider updating the kitchen and the washrooms. Laminate floors and ceramic tiles are easy to clean in the event the home becomes vacant. Consider also having the bathroom fan turn on automatically with the light to prevent mold. Even good tenants may not always remember to turn on the fan.

3.   Address all safety issues such as hard-wired smoke and carbon monoxide detectors.

4.   A good rental property should be one that is very easy to clean and upkeep for in-between tenancy. A well-maintained home will attract good tenants. A fresh coat of paint can really brighten up a dull home. After all, it is your investment, so protect it!

5.   It is better to buy small single-family homes instead of two-family ones. Mixing tenants can create problems because of different lifestyles. When choosing a tenant, choose a family instead of a group of adults.

Multiple sources of income in a household, especially if they are in different fields and not working for the same company, is more diversified and therefore more reliable than one person with a high income.

A typical family will prefer to live near good schools and with proximity to employment, shopping centres and highways. Families with children at different levels of school will most likely remain in the rental property for a longer time.

A group of adults sharing accommodation will lead to more problems such as keeping the home clean and paying utilities. Student rentals can be more profitable but more problematic as well.

Most people avoid investing in residential real estate because they do not want to deal with the archetypical "tenant from hell". However, if you find the right tenants, you will enjoy the process.

I had a tenant who gave me nine cheques that bounced in one year and I eventually had to go through the entire process of eviction. The good news was that this tenant had been working for the same employer for the past 24 years and so it was possible to get my money back by having the tenant's wages garnished.

I had another tenant who did an overnight move to skip out on rent. They had a backlog of three months payment and told me that they had just cashed in their RRSP and would pay me soon.

When I went over, they were gone! This tenant was working for a large food manufacturer as a Shipper/Receiver for the past five years. To cover the debt, I garnished their wages. The lesson here: job stability is more important than credit.

While many self-employed are great, some "professional tenants" might claim they are self-employed because they know it is difficult to garnish their wages upon default. Also, check whether outstanding rent can be pursued through a Small Claims Court in your jurisdiction. (As of January 1, 2020, the Ontario Small Claims Court will hear cases seeking payment of up to $35,000).

Some tenants outsmart novice landlords. Many will create a company overnight. I remember an occasion when a "CEO" arrived from the United States and wanted to rent a luxury home. His truck was packed and he needed to move immediately. He provided us with his financial statements and everything looked great until he moved in. It was an expensive lesson because the documents were manufactured. It is difficult to verify credit information and job references from a foreigner. The rent cheques returned NSF (Not Sufficient Funds) and it took a while to evict him. The landlord lost over $20,000.

The ideal tenant will have a clean credit and a stable job. However, over the years I've come to realize that in a matter of time, they will move on. Why should they pay rent when they can buy their own home? I've also had tenants who have a stable job but had their home repossessed by their lender, their credit damaged and no one wanted to rent to them. With their past experiences, these tenants did not want to move and they became good long-term tenants. A tenant with a bruised credit and a stable job is more likely to stay than a tenant with good credit and a stable job.

A prospective tenant told me that she went through a very difficult divorce and wanted to rent for a year. She would pay for the whole year's rent in advance. She was unemployed but had received a huge settlement from her recent divorce. It turned out that this individual was involved in a string of marijuana grow operations. By paying a year's rent in advance, we would not be in touch too often and she would have free reign to run her illegal grow op.

I had an application from a prospective tenant who claimed that he was employed with the same company for four years. I made a call to the company. The manager answered the phone and confirmed the employment. However, when I googled the address, it turned out to be a residential property. The job letter, pay stub and the employer were all fake. Always double-check employment history. Sometimes you can get this from the credit report. Ask for pay stubs, T4 slips and tax returns. More hoops to jump through will weed out uncertain tenants and individuals willing to commit fraud.

Once, I had two applicants for the same home. One applicant was making over $60,000 a year but his partner was not working. The other applicant was making $28,000 a year and his other half was earning $34,000. I choose the latter. All else equal, more people working, especially if they are in different fields, are better than one person with a high income.

One of the first questions I ask is when they would like to move in. Families tend to plan and make decisions at least a few months in advance. The ones who already have their trucks packed and are waiting to move in immediately might have been recently evicted.

Usually when a prospective tenant wants to view a property, I ask them a simple question: How many of you will be living here? Based on their answer, I ask to meet all of them, including the children, at the rental property. By meeting the family, I can quickly assess them. Like a detective, look at the bond between the parents and the children. These clues are valuable in assessing your prospective tenants. I had someone who once told me that she did not have any pets and yet her clothes were covered in cat hair. Another person told me that cleaning is one of his priorities, but the back seat of his car was full of used coffee cups.

Good tenants are the cornerstone for a rewarding real estate investment career. One of my tenants has lived in the same home for over eight years. They shovel the snow, do the landscaping and take excellent care of the home. The family is proud to be there. They owned a home before but had to sell it because of financial difficulty. In eight years, they have paid about $150,000 in rent.

When I search for a good tenant, I always look for someone who will take care of my property. I look for mature families who have jobs. In ten years, with each of my rental properties the mortgage principal was reduced, and the value appreciated. With the equity building up, I can buy other properties and find other great tenants. With long term tenants, however, there is a disadvantage. With recent rent escalation, I have many underpaying properties. For example, a home that would fetch $3,000 in rent only brings in $1700. I can only increase the rent as per the rental guidelines. While this is not ideal from a cash flow perspective, when you consider the capital appreciation over the ten years, the rent paid and the fact that they are taking care of the property, it's a headache free investment.

Real estate investing is one of the best vehicles for building wealth. With a completed rental application, credit check and proper screening, you can choose the right tenant. It is better to spend time upfront screening your tenants than to spend time later trying to evict them.

CHECKLIST FOR TENANTS

- ☐ Rental property upgraded between rentals
- ☐ Criteria established for evaluating desirable tenants
- ☐ Financial and employment background verified, and credible references obtained

☐ Debt to income ratio analyzed to determine their ability to pay. (The higher the debt to income, the less ability to pay).

☐ Plan in place to pursue rent arrears through legal means (if tenant is employed wage/salary garnishment is possible in some jurisdictions).

4.05 INCOME TAX IMPLICATIONS

There are many tax implications in the rental of an investment property. Generally, all amounts expended in the process of earning rental income are deductible from that income. [For more in-depth information applicable to your own jurisdiction, always consult a professional tax accountant, such as a CPA.]

The following should be kept in mind:

1. You can claim a depreciation allowance [percentage varies by location and type of property], otherwise referred to as a "Capital Cost Allowance", on the declining value of the property every year. This "allowance" is treated as a deduction from the rental income. The reader should be aware there are "claw back" implications if the property is a partial rental and the property is eventually sold. [Consult your CPA if in doubt].

2. The equity in the home, if reused for investment, is tax exempted and the interest payment on the mortgage or Line of Credit is a deductible expense from the income. Other major expenses considered as deductible from rental income include:

- Property tax

- Maintenance and repairs (providing these don't fall under the category of "capital improvements" which increase the value of the property)

- Property management expenses

- Property insurance

- Utilities (if paid by the landlord)

3.   If your rental income is less than your expenses, then that loss can be carried forward and deducted from future years' rental income. Later in life you can pay yourself a stable income from your investments. Other investments may not be able to generate a stable income when you are ready for it.

My formula is simple; buy, hold and profit—you are not cashing in your rental properties. If, however, you choose to sell, then fifty percent of the capital gain (in Canada) is yours to keep. The other fifty percent is taxable at your marginal rate. Check with your CPA for more insight into capital gains which can differ from jurisdiction to jurisdiction.

CHECKLIST FOR RENTAL PROPERTY AND INCOME TAX

- [ ] Up to date records kept of all rental income and expenses incurred in earning that income, along with supporting documentation

- [ ] Expenses related to the rental property are identifiable and distinct from personal expenses

☐ Separate bank accounts kept for each property

☐ Tax implications of rental income and allowable expenses discussed with a CPA

4.06 SHORT TERM RENTALS

Short-term rentals, such as *Airbnb's,* can be lucrative, fetching an average of about $150 daily in some jurisdictions. It is a boon for many. Millions of hosts and travelers around the world are benefitting from short-term rentals. The host enjoys the extra income and the guest welcomes affordable accommodation.

I rented a suite in London, England for a week and the service was excellent. The two-bedroom flat was beautifully furnished, and the price was below that of the local hotels. There are, however, horror stories in which the host's home is left trashed after a visit from rowdy guests. Airbnb's "Host Guarantee" program will cover the cost to a maximum of one million dollars, but the homeowner is not fully exempted.

Be sure to check with the mortgage and insurance companies before venturing into short-term rentals, lest you accidently breach a condition of the mortgage agreement or void your insurance.

HOW TO GET INTO SHORT TERM RENTALS

1.   A place that is well presented and nicely furnished will get great reviews

2.   It is best to register with a reputable company such as Airbnb, rather than to advertise independently

3.   Appealing photography of the premises and a virtual tour are imperative

4.   At first, there will be no reviews of the rental property, therefore the price should be set at below market value. Positive reviews are golden and will increase the rental potential

RULES GOVERNING SHORT TERM RENTALS

A short-term rental applies only to the principal residence where the owner-operator can rent a portion of the home, to a maximum of 3 bedrooms, for less than 28 consecutive days and must not exceed 180 days in a calendar year.

To qualify, the operator must have a license granted by the city and pay Municipal Accommodation Tax (MAT). The licensing authorities must have satisfactory evidence that the property is the owner's principal residence.

As an owner-operator, a guest must be able to contact you at any time during their stay. The guest must be advised on the proper use of an emergency call (9-1-1 in North America). All guests must be given a layout of the dwelling equipped with the nearest exits in case of an emergency (e.g., fire). Operators must keep a record of every short-term rental for a period of 3 years.

The record must include:

- The length of the stay

- Cost

- Whether the rental is for an entire unit or for a single room

Failure to comply with the rules may result in fines up to $100,000.

Condos are great avenues for short-term rentals as well. In this setting, guests have access to several amenities such as the concierge services, pool, gym and parking during their stay. However, most condos have rules disallowing short-term rentals and it is smart to review the condo declaration before proceeding.

Violating the rules of the condominium can result in stiff financial penalties levied against the owner. If a renter plans to rent an apartment on a short-term basis, be sure to check the lease. Most leases have restrictions against short-term rental and sublets. Violating the lease can even result in forcing the owner to sell. Further, if there are damages, the owner is personally liable.

IMPLICATIONS FOR SHORT-TERM RENTALS

- The income from short-term rentals is taxable

- By offering your home as a short-term rental, the owner is considered self-employed

- The rental income can be offset by expenses reasonably incurred to earn that income including:

  - Repairs

  - Supplies

  - Cleaning services

  - Advertising and promotion

  - Equivalent portion of mortgage interest, property tax and insurance

- Short-term rentals can be lucrative but require attention. A service provider must work to keep customers happy. One bad review can ruin the reputation of the property

- The owner must be accessible and have maintenance personnel on call

- The owner of the property will be living in close quarters with strangers and is essentially at their beck and call

- It is recommended that one go with a reputable company such as Airbnb

- Along with the risks, the rewards are high

The recent pandemic took a toll on short term rentals. Many investors who rely on this as a source of income were devastated. The best cherries are on the end of the weakest branches so be careful!

CHECKLIST FOR SHORT TERM RENTALS

- ☐ Cost benefit analysis done on short-term rental versus long term leasing
- ☐ Condominium rules do not prohibit short-term rental
- ☐ Tax implications have been considered
- ☐ Reputable company engaged
- ☐ Marketing portfolio established
- ☐ Advertising plan in place

SECTION V: LOOKING AHEAD

5.01 GLOBAL WARMING

The multi-million-dollar question today: What will be the impact of global warming on real estate values? Furthermore, what can we do to prepare for it?

Waterfront properties have always been and continue to be in demand. Some of the most expensive pieces of residential and commercial real estate all over the world are near beaches and lakes. It seems to conjure a feeling of excitement to be near water, and we all want a piece of the action. With global warming, however, the tides are changing. Consider that if these properties go underwater, or the land begins to subside, they may one day be worth less than the mortgage owing, resulting in negative equity.

IMPACT ON REAL ESTATE

With global warming, we are now experiencing more floods, hurricanes and forest fires. Oceanfront property values could drop substantially due to this. Ontario is no exception. Lakefront properties comprise some of the most expensive pieces of real estate and could be at risk.

As the earth warms, there is more evaporation and heavier rainfall. On July 19th, 2013, just within three hours, Toronto was flooded, sending the transit system in disarray. The sewer system could not handle the flow and countless basements were flooded, causing millions of dollars in damages. The government implemented new measures, changing building codes to require the installation of backflow valves and sump pumps.

I came across a shopping plaza in Muskoka with over 40,000 sq. feet of retail space. It was situated at the edge of a river which served as a drainage for stormwater. The rising water level created a problem. Part of the solution was to install new drains higher up, above the frost line. In the winter, these drains must be heated, resulting in increased electricity bills.

The cost of maintenance ballooned and was transferred to the tenants who could not afford it and eventually relocated. The once thriving plaza became an empty shell resulting in losses of millions of dollars.

Even if not in flood zones, the greenhouse effect damages property values near lake front properties. Ohio State University did a study in 2017 and found that home values near Buckeye Lake and Grand Lake decreased by $152 million from 2009 to 2015 because of inordinate algae growth. Communities in affected areas would lose some of their residences and businesses.

With a smaller population and diminished tax base, property tax would increase because fewer residences must carry the burden to run the city.

PREPARING FOR THE FUTURE

Some property owners are cashing in on the opportunity. They have sold their waterfront properties and bought cheaper properties in-land. A few families I know sold their lakefront cottages and used the proceeds to buy investment properties in Toronto.

It was a smart move for the future since they received a premium for their cottages and premium rent for their investment properties. They are on higher ground, so to speak.

In December 2019, Australia suffered the effects of climate change. The warm weather dried up the atmosphere and created drought-like conditions. This sparked a forest inferno and then the heavy clouds came pouring on soil that was too dry to absorb water. Scientists call this "compound extremes" where one climate disaster triggers the next. The financial cost to rebuild skyrocketed and farms were decimated. With forest fires, it becomes almost a certainty that home values on lovely ravine lots decrease in value.

Paradoxically, hurricanes can cause home values to increase. After a hurricane, the cost of building materials can climb. With a shortage of properties, rental rates surge and with fewer homes available for sale, home prices increase. Always keep in mind that price is driven by both supply and demand. Homes that are badly damaged create opportunities for investors who can purchase for little, rebuild and profit. While hurricanes benefit a fraction of people, many families without hurricane insurance will suffer.

Insurance cost is on the rise and many insurance companies have disclaimers, exclusions and high deductibles. Basic home insurance may not cover for floods, hurricanes or any natural disasters. A homeowner may need regular home insurance, flood insurance and hurricane insurance. Review your policy carefully so that you know what you are buying and ask a broker if you are still unsure whether your needs have been met. I recall an incident where the insurance company denied a claim for a hurricane because the policy states that "If the hurricane has a name, then the insurance company will not cover the cost."

With global warming rendering swathes of land uninhabitable, people will be concentrated in smaller areas. With population growth and longer life spans, the demand for prime real estate is greater. We may not live to see the full effects of global warming, but future generations will. While we are building wealth and transferring it to the next generation, let us give them a cleaner earth. Let's do our part.

CHECKLIST FOR GLOBAL WARMING

- ☐ Property is located outside the area of a floodplain

- ☐ Property has not been affected by natural disasters

- ☐ IF Property is subject to natural disasters, my insurance company confirmed coverage in writing

- ☐ Any new government regulations such as installation of back-flow valves and sump pumps, for recovery from natural disasters, have been complied with. (Failure to follow government mandates may also void your insurance so compliance is essential).

- ☐ If potential for damage from a natural disaster exists for my investment, an analysis has been done on the cost/ benefit of divesting and transferring the investment to something safer

5.02 SNOWBIRDS AND REAL ESTATE

The winter season spurs thousands of snowbirds to fly south every year. Those who spend winters consistently in the same place may decide to invest in a second home rather than renting indefinitely. With ownership, they can travel light, knowing that their home is fully equipped, with family portraits to their favourite pillows. Building wealth is an ongoing event and even at retirement, we can continue to invest.

ACQUIRING PROPERTY OUTSIDE CANADA

1.   Start by looking at various financial options for sourcing capital:

    a. Refinance the Canadian home and buy the vacation home in cash.

    b. Financing using a Canadian bank conducting business in that country.

2.   Ask for referrals from others who've bought. Their experiences are vital, and they can refer you to a local lawyer, realtor and lender. In places like Florida, with a thirty percent down payment, a buyer can secure financing. In addition to the down payment, the buyer must add about two percent of the

value of the property for cash purchase and five percent for properties with a mortgage.

3.   When shopping around for a home, first consider location, then size, and then upgrades. You can always upgrade or renovate a bigger home, but it is difficult and more cost intensive to extend a smaller one.

4.   Look for proximity to shops and public transportation. Look at statistics such as neighborhood population growth and income level. If the neighborhood population growth and income level are strong, it is a good investment. If instead you find the population is in decline and income levels are low, the property's value will probably fall.

5.   Before purchasing, spend about two months renting to know the neighborhood.

THINGS TO WATCH FOR

1.   Avoid beach-front properties. These are expensive and with climate change, can be targets for flooding and hurricanes. Insurance costs are higher and may not cover certain natural disasters. With rising sea levels, beach front properties will depreciate over time. Consult with a local insurance broker before deciding.

2.   For resale homes, knock on a few doors around the potential property and meet the neighbors. Ask the realtor to research what similar homes sold for within the last ninety

days so that you can make an informed decision. Prior to purchase, meet with the owners. They will know the property better than any realtor. Always submit an offer subject to financing, inspection and lawyer's approval.

3.   When buying a newly built home, research the builder and have a local lawyer review the agreement. A lawyer will ascertain whether there are any contractor liens or other encumbrances on the property. For example, if the roofing company was not paid by the main contractor, they can register a lien on the property. A supplier can also register a construction lien.

4.   Some buyers may prefer to live in a gated community where services such as security and lawn maintenance are included but buyers should realize that association fees can be high. There might also be restrictions against renting the property for extra income when the owner is away.

OTHER CONSIDERATIONS

1.   Use your interactions with lenders as a litmus test before buying. For example, if lenders refuse to finance based on a specific type such as time-shared properties, then do not buy.

2. Buyers must consider tax implications. Depending on how much time is spent in the U.S. and Canada, the individual may be taxed differently. Always check with a CPA for tax implications.

3. If we choose to rent the property when we are away, then the rental income is subject to thirty percent withholding tax unless done correctly. Again, it is important to consult a professional.

If done with careful preparation, snowbirds can bask in the sun on the sandy shores while their investments blossom.

As owners, remember your friends who may want to spend time with you at your new properties. However, it can become overwhelming. Let's take Ben Franklin's advice: "Guests, like fish, begin to smell after three days."

CHECKLIST FOR FOREIGN PURCHASES

☐ Most feasible and economical financing explored

☐ Research and background check done before buying

☐ Professional help engaged:

    ○ Legal council

    ○ Tax Accountant

    ○ Real estate salesperson

☐ Offer to Purchase is conditional on financing, inspection and lawyer's approval

5.03 SOLAR PANELS AND HOME VALUES

With more families becoming environmentally conscious, solar panels have increased in popularity. However, before venturing out on installing solar panels, do some research.

You can take advantage of solar energy if you live in a geographical area where sunlight is constant all year round. Ontario is the fourth sunniest province in Canada and homeowners are soaking it up by installing solar panels.

Solar panels are environmentally friendly and generate electricity for the home. Excess electricity is fed to the grid for a credit (check whether this applies to your jurisdiction). This system is called net metering where there is an adjustment between the amount of electricity sent to the grid and the amount used. Credit can only be carried forward for 12 months and then expires. The program is designed so that you cannot make money from your solar panels but only break-even.

The average cost to install solar panels for a typical detach home is between $20,000 to $25,000 and it will last for about twenty-five years. The system will pay for itself in fifteen years. In Ontario, there is no rebate on installation. [Check in your own jurisdiction for similar energy savings plans].

SOLAR PANELS—WHAT TO CONSIDER:

1. A south facing roof receives the most sunlight and generates more energy. Since solar panels last for about twenty-five years, replace the shingles before installation. Removing and re-installing solar panels can cost about $7,000.

2. Avoid installing solar panels on the front part of the roof because it takes away from the aesthetics.

3. Shop around and interview installers. Installers know how much electricity the system can produce based on the size, slope and direction of the roof.

4. Check the date of manufacture because newer versions are much more efficient than those even a few years older.

5. There might be two warranties — one from the manufacturer and the other from the installer. Find out.

6. If you are planning on leasing the system, make sure to have the contract reviewed by your lawyer before signing.

7. Check if any level of government provides rebates or incentives for installation

LEASING SOLAR PANELS

With leasing, you would have signed a contract to pay a monthly rent for the next 15 years or more. If you are selling the home and the buyers do not want to assume the lease, then you may have to pay an upfront cost for the remainder of the term plus removal cost and that can be substantial.

The lease should indicate who is responsible for the maintenance of the panel and in the event the panels must be removed and reinstalled.

IMPACT OF SOLAR PANELS ON PROPERTY

Does a solar panel really add value to your home? It depends on who you ask.

1.   Solar panel companies claim that it adds value to the property. In any jurisdiction, if it takes away from the aesthetics, then it takes away from the resale value. The value of a home depends first on location, then the size and last, the amenities.

2.   Installing a new kitchen and upgrading the washrooms are more desirable options for buyers than solar panels. Some buyers might request that the solar panel be removed, and the roof repaired prior to closing.

3.   With solar panels, the insurance cost will increase.

4.   Sales Tax (HST in Canada) on the electricity bill is charged on the gross consumption and not the net. [Check how handled in your jurisdiction]

5.   Solar panels also provide shelter for birds and animals and their droppings will damage the roof, resulting in premature replacement cost to the homeowner.

BUYING A HOUSE WITH SOLAR PANELS

Buyers purchasing homes with solar panels must complete their due diligence.

1.   Find out if the system is leased and if so, review the contract with someone knowledgeable about solar panels.

2.   Look at the seller's hydro bills for a year to see how the system performs. In the summer with long hours of sunlight, the system will outperform compared to winter when sunlight is limited and nights are longer.

Adding solar panels is a personal choice and should not necessarily be considered as a means of increasing the value of your home. If you will live in your home for a very long time, then consider investing in solar panels.

CHECKLIST FOR SOLAR PANELS

☐   Cost/benefit analysis done by a financial analyst to determine if installing solar panels will result in a net return over the period of the lease

☐ Legal advice obtained on the Lease/ Contract

☐ Company installing the panels has been checked out
with BBB and/ or other agencies

☐ Evaluation done on impact of panels on the future
(resale) value of the property determined that they
will not subtract from the appreciation and value

5.04 HOME RENOVATIONS

Home renovation is an essential item when investing in real estate. If it's a family home, then you can splurge a little. After all, you deserve it. However, if it is an investment property, then, be objective.

Most of the problems are caused because there is no contract in place. Usually, the contractor will come over, give an estimate and collect a deposit, after which the home renovations are officially underway.

Renovations, for many, are like marriage, honeymoon and then divorce. I usually tell my clients that contractors have legs and can run. The house does not have any legs and cannot run. Contractors, if not paid, can put a lien on the home but if you paid the contractor upfront and he did not finish the job, then it may prove difficult to run after them. It's best to give a deposit and pay as the job progresses. The frequency of payment should be documented in the contract.

ESSENTIALS FOR HOME RENOVATIONS

1. The best way is to plan, knowing what you are expecting to achieve. If you are

upgrading the kitchen, for example, you should know the kind of cupboards, countertop, backsplash, range hood, and floor needed.

2.   For major renovations, such as finishing a basement or re-modeling, consult an architect. I remodeled my kitchen and realized after that the cupboards for pots and pans were too small, but by then it was too late to change anything. Had I consulted an architect, the outcome could have been different.

3.   If it is a major renovation, check with the city. You may need a permit.

4.   City inspectors are there to ensure that the job is done according to building codes. They are like the police for contractors. I learned the hard way when I hired a contractor to install pot lights in my home. After the job was finished, I insisted on having the Electrical Safety Authority inspect it. It turned out that most of the work was done wrong. I engaged another electrician to clean up the mess at my own expense. Had I applied for the permit in the first place, the safety authority would have overseen the project

5.   The next step is to look at the financial framework. If you are renovating the bathroom, what is your budget? What will it cost you for porcelain tiles and quartz countertop, versus regular ceramic tiles and

laminate counters? The cost of labour might be the same, but the choice of materials can make a major difference once finished.

6.   It is best to choose your own materials and pay for labor separately. If the contractors' cost includes materials, they may settle for cheaper products.

7.   Always over-budget the project by 10% to 15%. Know the cost of renovations and arrange financing.

8.   Before you proceed, interview many contractors and seek quotes. Contractors can share remodeling ideas from different work sites.

9.   Ask contractors for written quotes and the time frame to complete the work. Some contractors will complete one project at a time while others may work on various job sites at the same time. Choose one that will work on your project full time.

10.   Check references and visit a few of their previous projects. If possible, chat with the homeowners.

11.   Once you choose a contractor, ask for a detailed contract that includes the scope of the work, start and finish date and the cost.

12.   If the contract is detailed or the project includes subcontractors, consider having your lawyer review and explain to you the sections on warranties, insurance and indemnity.

13. Ask for a copy of the contractor's Workers Compensation Insurance or similar coverage so that you're protected if there's an accident on site. You may also want a copy of their commercial general insurance policy along with information about the policy limits.

14. Discuss the terms of payment ahead of time. Start with a partial payment up front and pay as the job progresses (ideally at times specified in the contract). If the contractor insists on getting paid up front, that's a red flag.

PREPARING FOR THE PROJECT

- Renovating is a dusty, dirty job. It begins with demolition before the re-modeling can occur

- Put away valuables because strangers will have access to your home

- Remove pictures from the walls and cover furniture

- If it is a large project, consider storing the furniture

- Cover the floor with cardboard sheets for protection

- If it is summer, turn off the AC and cover the vents, otherwise change the furnace filter frequently

- If it is a condo, then contact management before you start because they may have restrictions

Avoid the temptation of overspending. Choose renovations that will enhance the value of your home, and be realistic.

CHECKLIST FOR HOME RENOVATIONS

- ☐ Objectives clearly defined

- ☐ Budget prepared for project

- ☐ Ten or fifteen percent overrun included in the budget

- ☐ Financing available or arranged

- ☐ Architect consulted for major renovation plans such as structural or other design changes

- ☐ At least three reputable contractors contacted

- ☐ References obtained for contractors

- ☐ Written contract/agreement signed with details of project along with associated costs

- ☐ Workers Compensation or similar policy on record

- ☐ Percentage of completion agreed to for (partial) payment(s).

- ☐ Holdback enshrined for eventualities

SECTION VI: TRANSITIONING

6.01 REVERSE MORTGAGES

Many of us, in our golden years, are house rich but cash poor. A reverse mortgage can be a viable option to enjoy some of the wealth otherwise locked in on our home.

ASPECTS OF A REVERSE MORTGAGE

Reverse mortgages are created especially for seniors so they can release equity from their homes without having to sell. The amount of equity that is made available depends on:

- The age of the homeowner
- The value of the home
- Other terms specified by the lender

The loan is paid back with interest when the borrower either sells the property, moves out or passes away. Where there are two owners, such as a matrimonial home, that privilege is extended to the surviving spouse.

BENEFITS OF A REVERSE MORTGAGE

1.   Justin and Ava are retired. They have been living in their family home for over twenty

years. Their home is worth $900,000 and they have a remaining mortgage of $50,000. They love their home but with limited income and a shoestring budget, it is becoming increasingly difficult to maintain their lifestyle. Their options are to sell their home and move or get a reverse mortgage. They chose the latter. With this option, Justin and Ava don't have to leave the comfort of their home, and at the same time they supplement their monthly income.

2.   Many seniors are also living longer and prefer to reside at home, considering the impact of a pandemic such as Covid. Over time, if the value of the home increases, their equity increases. With a reverse mortgage, they can enjoy an affluent lifestyle without having to sell or move from their property.

3.   Unlike a traditional mortgage where you pay the lender, in a reverse mortgage the lender pays you based on a percentage of your home's overall value. Since it is equity from their principal residence, it is not considered as income and is not taxable. It does not affect their old age security income. They can accept one lump sum payment or take it in monthly installments.

DISADVANTAGES

1.   On reverse mortgages, the interest rate is usually higher than a conventional

mortgage. The cost associated in arranging a reverse mortgage exceeds that for a conventional one

2.   The equity in the home will erode over time. This can result in a heavier financial burden in the future. In some instances, the debt owing ends up being more than the value of the home.

3.   In the event of death, the estate must repay the loan plus interest over a specific period which might be shorter than the time needed to settle the estate and can cost substantially higher with penalties and discharge fees.

TYPICAL REQUIREMENTS FOR A REVERSE MORTGAGE

- Homeowners must be 55 years or older

- The property must be their principal residence

- If there is a mortgage on the property, it must be paid off. This can, however, be done with the cash advance received from the reverse mortgage

- The owner cannot secure any other debts such as a line of credit or second mortgage on the property

The reverse mortgage will become the *new* first mortgage on the property. The lender will lend to a maximum of 55% of the appraised value of the home. In this example, with the reverse mortgage, they are qualified for $495,000 in total mortgage against the property. Since there is a current mortgage of $50,000, the lender would lend $445,000 in one lump sum payment or arrange a monthly payment plan where Justine and Ava can supplement their income.

COSTS INVOLVED

The cost involved in arranging a reverse mortgage varies depending on the lender:

- Appraisal fee

- Lawyer's fees

- Setup charges

- Most reverse mortgages are insured at the borrower's expense

Borrowers must consider the interest charged and the penalties acquired for paying off the loan before the due date. It is important to consult a real estate lawyer before making a commitment.

Reverse mortgages are offered by various financial institutions (in Canada, under the CHIP—Canadian Home Income Plan, there are two main providers: Equitable Bank and Home Equity Bank). The borrower must maintain the property and keep up with insurance, property taxes and utilities. Although payments are not needed until a mortgage due date, a borrower will have prepayment privileges. Any prepayment privileges will be applied first towards penalties, then interest and last to the principal.

According to the Canadian Office of the Superintendent of Financial Institutions (OSFI), as of December 2019, debts from reserve mortgages top $4 billion. The baby boomers are becoming seniors and many do not have a pension plan—all their wealth is tied up into their homes.

ALTERNATIVES TO A REVERSE MORTGAGE

- Sell the property and buy something cheaper, thereby freeing up cash

- Arrange a regular mortgage

- Take out a line of credit

Whichever alternative is taken, the proceeds should be invested carefully to generate an income stream. Some seniors use the proceeds to build a basement apartment, while others invest in stocks and second mortgage loans. Use trusted advisers to evaluate the options before adopting one.

Reverse mortgages provide a viable path for seniors who do not have enough money to enjoy retirement. However, it is a more expensive option and if we are blessed with a long life, we may end up with less money than planned.

CHECKLIST FOR REVERSE MORTGAGES

- ☐ Options reviewed: sell, refinance or obtain a Reverse Mortgage on the property
- ☐ Professional Financial Analyst consulted for best option
- ☐ Budget prepared to consider current and future cash flow needs if:
    - o equity to be paid out in lump sum, or
    - o monthly
- ☐ Financial Analyst consulted for best investment option(s) if equity paid in lump sum
- ☐ Upfront cost and its impact clearly explained
- ☐ Amortization schedule supplied and shows the real cost of borrowing over the period of the Reverse Mortgage

6.02 WHY TRANSITION?

While time and good decisions compound wealth, we must always remember that our time on Earth is finite. Estate planning is an important ingredient in wealth preservation.

Estate planning can be simple or intricate—it depends on many factors. If estate planning involves the family home and a few other assets, a Will is sufficient. If it involves multiple investments such as real estate, stocks, and other assets, then planning may be a bit more complicated.

While laws vary from jurisdiction to jurisdiction, upon death, the deceased's assets are deemed to have been disposed of. If a Will exists, the money will belong to the estate less debts, probate fees and taxes. Life insurance and a Registered Retirement Savings Plans [RRSPs in Canada] are not part of your estate and are not subjected to probate fees. RRSPs can be transferred to a spouse, tax-free [in Canada]. Other than that, it is taxable. A permanent life insurance is a good idea to have because the proceeds can be used to pay probate fees, taxes and other obligations. However, a policy can be costly.

PRE-PLANNING TRANSITION OF THE ESTATE

1.   Although life is unpredictable, it is best to begin disposing of most assets before death. An investment property, for example, once sold or transferred to a family member, will trigger capital gains. With capital gains, 50% of the profit is considered income (in Canada) and will be taxed according to your marginal rate [Check with your Accountant].

2.   Dispose of the assets gradually, especially when your taxable income is low. However, if an investment property is gifted to a child, note that capital gains are calculated based on the true value of the property at the time it was gifted.

3.   The principal residence is exempted but if left in a Will, it will be subject to probate fees. Another idea is to add a family member as a joint tenant. In the event of death, the entire property will be held by the survivor. Joint assets are not part of the estate and are not subject to probate fees.

4.   Another option is to create a family trust. A family trust is created when you equitably give property to another person—the trustee, to keep in custody for the eventual benefit of a third party (here, a family member). When you create a family trust, you give up ownership to the trustee and that will trigger capital gains on your investment assets.

[Check with your Banker and CPA for up-to-date tax treatment]

Life is a speeding torrent, racing down a steep hill, and no one wants to think about death. However, we've all heard the adage that the only certainties in life are death and taxes. You work hard for your money and want most of it to be in the hands of your loved ones. Careful estate planning can accomplish that.

CHECKLIST FOR TRANSITIONING

- ☐ A detailed list of all assets and liabilities documented
- ☐ Beneficiaries clearly specified for all assets
- ☐ Consulted with Accountant/ Lawyer/ Financial Adviser for tax implications and best options:
    - ○ Transition at death through a Will or
    - ○ Family Trust for future income treatment
- ☐ Plan in place for transition

6.03 WILLS AND WHAT'S INVOLVED

What happens when a loved one dies?

At my secondary school, in the auditorium there was a banner that read: *Those who fail to plan must plan to fail.* It is human nature to postpone making our Will because we believe that we are not ready for death. A Will dictates how our assets are distributed upon death and should be prepared at the earliest opportunity and revised periodically.

PROBATING THE WILL

Probate is when the executor of the Will applies to the court for a *Certificate of Appointment.* (In Ontario, an estate trustee is the only person with legal authority to manage an estate). By probating the Will, you are providing a person with the authority to act as the estate trustee. The average wait time for this is about four to six months and if the court is backlogged, it can take a year or more.

CERTIFICATE OF APPOINTMENT

I've encountered situations where a home is sold before obtaining the *Certificate of Appointment.* In these situations, the Sales Agreement must have a postponement clause which states that if the Certificate of Appointment is not received, the seller has the right to postpone closing to a later date when the certificate is granted. If this clause is not in the Agreement and on the closing date the Certificate is not granted, the seller will be in default and liable to the buyers for damages.

If there is a mortgage on the property, chances are the mortgage payments are being made automatically from the account of the deceased. Executors should inform the institution that holds the mortgage and arrange to make payments, if needed.

COSTS TO CONSIDER PROBATING THE WILL

• Estate administration tax of about 1.5% [depending on the jurisdiction] of the value of the estate. The family realtor can give a written estimate of the value of the home and might advise against putting the home on the market until the Certificate of Appointment has been received.

• Lawyer's fees

• Probate fees

• Unpaid property tax, mortgages, etc.

• Executor fees

PREPARING FOR THE TRANSFER OF ASSETS

1.   Estate planning is essential and the first place to start is with a Will. Dwayne owned four rental properties, and all were in his name in addition to one of his four children's, making each a joint tenant. Joint tenancy is between two or more people and if one party dies, the property will automatically transfer into the name of the survivor(s).

2.   If the properties were in Dwayne's name alone, then they would have formed part of the estate and would have been subjected to an Estate Administration Tax. In addition, upon death, the properties would have been deemed "disposed", meaning that they would be changing hands and automatically trigger capital gains tax (in Canada). By adding his children on title as joint tenants, Dwayne's children saved on Capital Gains Tax [valid in Canada—check if this applies in your jurisdiction]. A Family Trust serves the same purpose and at the same time protects properties from creditors.

3.   After the Certificate of Appointment had been granted, Dwyane's sons William and Henry consulted with their realtor and sold one of the properties for much more than the original estimate. As executors, William and Henry had to file an Estate Information Return (in Ontario to the Ontario Ministry of Finance within ninety days from the time the certificate

was issued. Again, check what applies in your jurisdiction). The Estate Information Return is a list of all the assets, including details of all bank accounts, Registered Retirement Savings Plans (RRSPs), etc., that are part of the estate, to be able to assess its worth. At this point, the Estate administration tax must be paid. The executors are subjected to stiff penalties if they try to diminish the estate's true value to reduce tax owing.

4.   William and Henry worked with their accountant to file two tax returns. One for the part of the year Dwayne was alive and a second for the remainder of the fiscal year. The accountant also requested a Clearance Certificate from the Canadian Revenue Authority [check your own jurisdiction for the appropriate tax authority]. There were some unpaid taxes and other penalties imposed and once that was paid, William and Henry received the final tax clearance. At this point, the assets from the estate were disposed of as directed by the will.

While the time of death is uncertain, death itself is. As such, the earlier we prepare a Will, the better.

ESSENTIAL ELEMENTS IN A WILL (check with a competent authority for more information on your jurisdiction)

- A Will must be in writing to be legal and the person who creates the document must be of sound mind and at least eighteen years old

- The document must have the name and address of the creator of the Will. The author of the Will must state the executor(s) responsible for settling the estate. Always choose an alternative executor to provide for contingencies. Provide the name and address of the executor(s) and alternate executor as well. Your executor becomes liable to pay off all debts and settle the estate

- The Will must state the beneficiaries and dictate what asset should be given to which beneficiary. The name and address of the beneficiaries is important

- The Will must have detailed instructions as to *how much* and *when* the beneficiaries are entitled to their inheritance

- Since there may be other items missing from the list of assets, it is a good idea to consider a clause stating that "the residue goes to..." and put the name and address of that person

- The Will must also address who will become the guardian(s) of any minor children or dependents

- Finally, the person must state that he or she is signing the Will and have two arms-length witnesses when signing

PREPARING A WILL

1.   Most lawyers can prepare a Will for under one thousand dollars. You can use a lawyer or your bank as the administrator too. Their fees typically range between 2% to 4% of the estate; this can be hefty. Your Will should be kept in a safe, secure place with the beneficiaries having full knowledge of it.

2.   If you have a large family and are planning on using your children as the administrators, avoid choosing all the members. If they disagree, it can create family disharmony and hold up finalization of the estate for a long time.

Upon death, the Will must pass probate court to ensure that it is valid. The cost is about 1.5% of the estate [in Ontario; check applicability in your jurisdiction].

AVOIDING COMPLICATIONS

1.   One of my late clients made all five of her children as beneficiaries and executors of her estate. Her instructions on how the assets were to be distributed were not clear and tensions quickly arose among the children. Eventually, the courts were involved. It was an expensive ordeal that left all the family members with bitter sentiments and little inheritance.

2. It is better to assign two individuals to act as executors. Many choose to have someone independent from the family like a close friend, or a professional such as a lawyer or a financial institution. The fees can be negotiated.

IMPORTANT ASPECTS OF A WILL (Most of these provisions apply in Ontario. Check with a competent professional for your area to determine applicability).

• Not all instructions written in a Will must be carried out. Recently, a client called for a market evaluation of the property she was living in because of the death of her husband. It was his second marriage, and, in his Will, it stated that 25% of the value of the property was to be given to her and the other 75% to his children from his previous marriage. With some research, I discovered that the property was registered in joint tenancy between my client and her late husband. I advised her that with joint ownership, the property automatically transfers to her, the survivor, upon his death and would be excluded from the estate's assets to be distributed.

• In situations where there are legal duties such as supporting a child or a former spouse, a portion of the asset should be set aside for them. Failing which, the dependents can, with varying degrees of success, ask the court to alter the Will. Insurance policies and joint accounts already have beneficiaries and automatically do not qualify as inheritance.

- Common law spouses do not automatically receive all their spouse's assets unless there is a legal Will. If there is none, then the person dies intestate, and the assets will go to their heirs. For common law relationships, both parties must have independent Wills designating each other as beneficiaries.

- For married couples, if one spouse dies leaving assets that are not jointly owned to other family members, in absence of a Will, the other spouse can apply for "equalization." It is a similar process for a divorce where both parties get an equal share of the matrimonial assets. The other half will then be distributed in accordance with the Will. For equalization, it must be done within six months of death.

- There are costs associated with the execution of a Will and many times, the families are "estate rich and cash poor." It is smart to leave about 15% of the value of the estate with your executor to pay for settlement. Remember, everything must be in writing to be valid. However, not everything in writing will always be valid (joint tenancy and other aspects of property or family law may override the division of property contemplated by the Will). Always consult a professional to make sure your preferences are reflected in the Will.

CHECKLIST FOR WILLS

- ☐ The Will is the "Last Will and Testament" and clearly indicates this

- ☐ Distribution of net assets and payment of outstanding debts clearly provided for

- ☐ The Executor(s) have agreed to carry out the terms of the Will

- ☐ The Executor(s) are fully aware of their responsibilities and reimbursement for services

- ☐ The Executor(s) are aware of the location of the Will

6.04 FAMILY TRUSTS

A Family Trust is a three-party fiduciary relationship which is created by the "Settlor" (or "Grantor") to hold family assets and pass it on to the beneficiaries after death with the help of a "trustee" who oversees the transfer. It is also known as a Revocable Living Trust. *Revocable* means that the person who creates the document can change anything as desired or even cancel the trust. *Living* establishes the fact that the trust survives death.

Fizal owned four properties and, to save on estate taxes, opened a family trust. The trust stipulated that upon Fizal's death, two properties would go to each of his two children; the first property would be transferred on their fortieth birthday and the second on their sixtieth. Fizal was the trustee of the family trust and upon his death, his lawyer, for a pre-arranged fee, would act as the secondary trustee.

Transferring investment properties to a Family Trust is a deemed disposition, triggering capital gains tax. As such, Fizal transferred one property each year to avoid paying all the taxes at higher marginal tax brackets. To facilitate the transfer, Fizal signed a *Quit Claim Deed*, where he relinquished his claim of the property to the trustee.

ESSENTIALS OF A FAMILY TRUST

1. The family trust requires an easily identified name. Most people choose a family name, for example, "Ali's Family Trust". The trust details must have the name of the trustee and the successor trustee(s).

2. The last part of the document should have the names of the beneficiaries and their relationship to the settlor. It stipulates that the beneficiaries' share and what will happen if the beneficiaries die before the Settlor.

For example, Ali has two children, Rafie and Fazie—each designated to inherit 50% of Ali's estate. The trust agreement states that Fazie is the beneficiary of 50% *by representation*, meaning that 50% will go to his children. If the beneficiaries are instead addressed as *A Case That Closes*, then if one dies, their portion goes to the other.

3. For the family trust to be valid, it must be dated. It is a legal binding document between the settlor and the trustee and as such, both parties should have the trust notarized.

FAMILY TRUST: CREATION AND OPERATION

1.   Assets such as real estate, stocks and bonds, other investments, saving accounts and life insurance proceeds are transferred to a family trust.

2.   The family trust becomes a space where investments can grow and produce profits. While not a legal entity such as a corporation or an individual, it is a taxpayer, typically at the highest marginal rates under Canadian law. There are two types of beneficiaries: Income and Capital. Income Beneficiaries are entitled to receive income from the trust while Capital Beneficiaries receive capital either during the life of the trust or when the trust is closed.

3.   A family trust, once established with the correct terms, can pay for senior living and funeral expenses as well. The details can be reviewed and changed anytime when both the settlor and trustee agree.

Emma and Olivia established a family trust where upon retirement, they would both receive an income. They adopted a special-needs child, Aliya. Since they were both settlors as well as the trustees of the family trust, Emma and Olivia added Aliya as an income beneficiary when she turned 18 years old and if they died before Aliya's 18th birthday, the income would go to her caretaker. This clause was added under the beneficiary's details.

FAMILY TRUST: PROS AND CONS

1.   One of the major benefits is that your assets are protected against creditors of your beneficiaries. For example, if one of the beneficiaries receives wealth from the estate settlement, then creditors can file a claim. A businessperson may want to put his assets in a family trust and if the business goes sour, the assets are protected from personal bankruptcy.

2.   The family home can be transferred to the trust, but the former owner can still live there. Assets transferred to your children in a Will can become available to their partners, but in a Family Trust it is **not** considered as part of personal property and is not subject to claims of the children's partner. The disadvantage, however, is that you lose personal control and the beneficial rights to assets under the trust agreement.

CHECKLIST FOR FAMILY TRUSTS

☐   Objectives of creating a family trust clearly laid out

☐   Benefits and disadvantages explained by the following professionals:

    o   Lawyer

    o   Accountant

    o   Financial Adviser

☐ Operation of the trust is documented with clearly defined beneficiaries and how the income **and** capital will be handled

6.05 UNTYING THE KNOT

Tying the knot is sweet but untying it is sometimes bitter. In wealth preservation, it's an important topic to address.

While most enter matrimony with an expectation of permanency (i.e., "until death do us part"), marriages do sometimes break down, with serious financial and emotional implications.

I came across a cartoon of a cow being milked, a couple, and two lawyers, where one spouse was pulling the head of the cow in one direction and, the other, yanking at the tail. The lawyers sat in the middle milking away.

THE MATRIMONIAL HOME

The matrimonial home is usually the biggest asset and untying its knot can be tough. For a property to be considered a matrimonial home, the couple must be legally married (this does not include couples who are cohabitating and living together) and live in that home. It does not matter who is on the title. [Check in your jurisdiction for applicability].

If the home was an inheritance or gifted and is used as the family home, both spouses still have equal rights unless there is a written marriage agreement. For example, consider John who inherited $60,000 and used it to upgrade the family home. John tried to claim that amount back on separation with his spouse, when the home was sold, but lost because the inheritance was used to update the family home. If John had kept the $60,000 in a separate bank account, on separation, he would have been able to deduct this amount from the family assets to be split with his spouse.

HOW ASSETS ARE HANDLED IN A BREAKDOWN

1.   With divorce, there is equalization. Both parties will add up their assets, subtract their debts and arrive at their final net worth.

2.   The spouse with the higher net worth then gives half of the difference to the other. In Common Law, in many jurisdictions, what was yours before the union typically stays as yours.

[Check with a competent professional to see what applies in your jurisdiction].

FAMILY HOME: IMPLICATIONS ON ASSETS

Picture Jackie, whose divorce was bitter. She left her home three years ago, and her ex-husband, Shob, was arguing that the family home was no longer a matrimonial home. He was the only name on the title. Fortunately, Jackie and Shob had lived in the home for ten years prior to their separation and the court considered that as substantial. There are a few options when disposing of the family home in a situation like this. One spouse can buy out the other, or as an alternative the home can be sold. In some instances, both parties may elect to keep the home so that their children's lives are not disrupted.

If one party needs to buy out the other, then, they must be financially capable. Caroline planned on keeping the family home and would arrange to buy out her ex, Ricardo. The home was worth $600,000 with a remaining mortgage of $200,000. As such, for Caroline to buy the home over, she had to pay Ricardo $200,000 (house valued $600,000 less the mortgage balance of $200,000, balance of $400,000 divided in two). Her only option was to increase the mortgage to $400,000. Since Ricardo would be removed from the title, Caroline would need to qualify on her own. With a single income, higher mortgage payments and all the costs associated with homeownership, Caroline must be careful.

Avoid the temptation to resort to conflict during a separation. Avi's former spouse got a restraining order against him and so he could no longer visit the family home. Anita, with their two children, stayed in the family home. The court ordered Avi to pay the mortgage and property tax. He was fuming because in addition to the court order, he must pay for his accommodation elsewhere. Eventually, the court ordered the home to be sold but Anita was uncooperative. She deliberately kept the home dirty and less appealing and as a result, the home remained on the market for a longer period and sold well below market value. Avi and Anita both took a financial tumble.

Dan and David, on the other hand, untied the knot and sold their home. They ironed out a fair arrangement, interviewed a few realtors and sold their home. On moving day, they assisted each other, hugged and moved on. Dan and David are better off financially.

If both parties cannot agree to sell, then one party can apply for a court order. The proceeds of the sale will remain in the real estate lawyer's trust account until a settlement is reached.

It is smart to have a prenuptial or postnuptial agreement in place because we never know what the future holds.

CHECKLIST FOR UNTYING THE KNOT

- ☐ Cooling-off period negotiated with spouse
- ☐ Emotions taken out of the negotiations between spouses
- ☐ Professionals (lawyer and accountant) engaged for the dissolution
- ☐ Rights, obligations and responsibilities of both parties researched
- ☐ Prenuptial Agreement previously negotiated

6.04 GLOSSARY

ABATEMENT: in real estate, a reduction or an exemption for a home's property tax, usually offered as an incentive to the owner. For example: seasonal businesses may receive an abatement from the regular property tax.

ACCEPTANCE: when a buyer agrees to purchase a property under conditions set by the seller.

APPRAISAL: an estimate of the value of the property based on what similar properties recently sold for. With an appraisal, you can calculate the equity in the property. A licensed property appraiser would research the property through MLS (Multiple Listing Services).

ASSIGNEE: an individual or entity receiving property or title pursuant to the terms of a contract.

ASSIGNMENT: the transfer of property rights from an assignor to an assignee. The assignment of pre-construction condominium units is often permitted by contracts.

ASSIGNOR: the individual or entity conveying property or title pursuant to the terms of a contract.

BALANCE SHEET: a snapshot of your total assets and total liabilities at a particular point in time, likely at the end of your financial period. The difference between the two is your Equity or ownership value.

BENEFICIARY: person(s) who benefit/s from a distribution of an estate either through the terms of a Will or a Family Trust.

CASH FLOW: the amount of cash coming in from a property, especially from rental. NEGATIVE CASH FLOW: Where outflows or expenses exceed the cash (rental income). POSITIVE CASH FLOW is where cash coming in exceeds expenses.

CERTIFICATE OF APPOINTMENT: where the Executor(s) is/are granted the power to execute the terms of a Will.

CLOSING COSTS: the cost linked to the purchase or sale of a home such as sales tax, lawyer fees and lender fees, in addition to the down payment.

CLOSING DATE: the date when ownership/title and money change hands. Many steps must be taken simultaneously to reach this point in the transaction.

CMHC: Central Mortgage and Housing Corp [a government agency in Canada]. Protects the lender (institution financing the mortgage) in high ratio mortgages. The cost of the premiums is rolled into the mortgage. CMHC insurance can be avoided by making a down payment of at least 20% of the purchase.

COMMISSION: a fee paid to an employee for a service or transaction performed. When selling a home for example, the seller will pay a commission to the Realtor involved in that transaction.

CONDOMINIUM (CONDO for short): a building where the units are individually owned and common areas such as the roof, passageway and elevators, etc. share in joint ownership.

CREDIT REPORT: a report generated/ obtained from an approved Credit Reporting Agency, laying out the status of the credit worthiness of the person(s) in question.

DUE DILIGENCE (PERIOD): usually the Buyer's lawyer has a time frame to research the title of the property being purchased. This is known as "the due diligence period" and the deadline is called the requisition date.

EASEMENT: is a right of use (on a property) given to someone other than the homeowner.

EQUITY: is the value remaining after deducting the amount owed on the mortgage from the current sale price of the home.

EXECUTOR: the person appointed by someone to execute the terms of a Will.

FAMILY TRUST: (also known as a *Revocable Living Trust*) is a legal document created to hold the family assets and pass it on to the beneficiaries after death.

FINANCIAL PLAN: a plan drawn up with the objective of showing proposed income and expenses of a particular business undertaking. Might be prepared for a Financial Institution as a prerequisite for obtaining a loan.

FLIPPING: the process of purchasing and selling a property with the main objective of utilizing the upturn in market forces.

GARNISHMENT: a legal process where a court may order a third party, such as an employer to deduct an amount of money from an employee's paycheck and send that to another party. An example is when a tenant fails to pay rent, the landlord can apply to garnish a portion of the tenant's wage.

HELOC: Home Equity Line of Credit. An amount of credit extended by a financial institution with a portion of the equity in your house registered as collateral.

HOME INSPECTION: a process of inspecting a property to determine its flaws. Typically undertaken by a purchaser who will engage a professional.

HST: Harmonized Sales Tax [a blend of applicable Provincial Sales Tax and the Federal Sales Tax in Canada].

IRREVOCABILITY CLAUSE: the deadline set for the offer/ acceptance of the sale/ purchase of the property

LAND TITLE REGISTRY: the Registry is a government agency that transfers title in the property from the seller to the buyer.

LAND TRANSFER TAX: a sales tax paid when a purchaser buys real estate. Since a buyer cannot move the land (like other products such as a computer), it can only be transferred to the new owners. As such, it is called land transfer tax. It is calculated based on the sale price of the property.

LIENS: are registered claims against the property. They represent unpaid debts like property taxes from a previous owner or unpaid amounts for services performed on the property, like installation of windows or a furnace. Many contractors employ this method to guarantee payment for work done.

LINKED HOUSE: "a link detach". The foundation walls below ground are linked by two common walls running lengthwise along the entire stretch of homes. The cross-foundation walls are then constructed, and earth is thrown between the homes. Above ground, it looks like a detached, but below it is linked.

MORTGAGE: the outstanding balance due on a loan that was secured for the purpose of acquiring property.

MORTGAGE PAYMENT: the amount due in a specific agreed-to period as payment to the institution that financed the purchase of the property. Typically made up of principal plus interest on the outstanding balance. Interest is typically calculated as a larger portion of the payment, with a smaller amount going towards the principal in the early years and as the years accumulate the ratio of principal to interest switches.

MORTGAGE PREAPPROVAL AND PREQUALIFICATION: when a buyer is prequalified, it's only an estimate of how much she can afford. It does not investigate the finer details such as her credit and her ability to pay. PRE-APPROVAL, on the other hand, imposes such responsibilities where the buyer completes an application and all the necessary documentation for review. If successful, the lender would issue a commitment letter to the buyer.

NET OPERATING INCOME: total income less operating expenses for a particular project/business.

NET INCOME: total income less operating expenses and extraordinary items.

NET WORTH: total assets less total liabilities, as calculated on a Balance Sheet. Represents the amount of ownership in assets.

OFFER: is an agreement to purchase a property under specific conditions. This agreement is time sensitive and contains deadlines.

PARTNERSHIP: a legal agreement between two or more parties for the purpose of undertaking a business venture, either specific to an investment or open-ended.

PORTFOLIO: the total of assets and investments.

PRE-INSPECTION: at the pre-inspection phase, the home is investigated for imperfections and defects that need to be adjusted before occupancy.

PROBATING: as in a will. When the executor applies to the court for a Certificate of Appointment.

PROFIT AND LOSS STATEMENT: a financial document outlining income from various sources and the expenses incurred in earning such income, resulting in either a NET PROFIT or NET LOSS.

PROPERTY INFORMATION STATEMENT: a disclosure statement that the seller may have provided to the realtor. A history report can also be requested providing information if the home ever had an insurance claim for fire, flood, sewage back-up or if the property was used as a grow-up.

PROPERTY MANAGEMENT COMPANY: a company engaged in managing an investment property or properties for a fee, paid by the owner(s) of the property.

RATE OF RETURN/ RETURN ON INVESTMENT: a measure of whether it's worthwhile to proceed with an investment. Calculated as the net gain or loss on an investment over a specified period, expressed as a percentage of the investment's initial cost.

REAL ESTATE BUBBLE: when property prices climb rapidly to an unsustainable level and then crash.

RENT CONTROLS: in some jurisdictions, rents are not allowed to be raised beyond a certain percentage annually, often tied to an economic metric such as the rate of inflation.

RENT-TO-OWN: where a part of the rent paid goes towards the down payment for the tenant to eventually purchase the property.

RESERVE/ RESERVE FUND: the amount set aside as a contingency (by Condo Boards, for example) for a specific purpose or unexpected expenses. Required by law in some jurisdictions.

REVERSE MORTGAGE: a loan secured against a property. A regular mortgage can be called a forward mortgage where the borrower makes monthly payments. In a reverse mortgage, no monthly payment is required. When the borrower dies, moves permanently or sells the property, the lender is then repaid.

RRSP: Registered Retirement Savings Plan (in Canada). An amount allowed, within specific parameters, by the Federal Government as a deduction to arrive at your taxable income. Most likely called something different in other jurisdictions if allowed.

RRSP MORTGAGE: where the investor (in the RRSP) converts his RRSP into a mortgage on a specific property. This is called a private mortgage and the terms and conditions are negotiated by both the financial institution and the RRSP holder.

SECOND MORTGAGE: a mortgage taken out on a home that already has a mortgage (see MORTGAGE above). There are specific rules governing which mortgage has priority.

SECURED LINE OF CREDIT: a loan obtained from a financial institution and secured with real property, such as a home. The cost of borrowing is generally lower than that of a conventional loan. (See also HELOC)

SELLER TAKE BACK MORTGAGE: a private mortgage where the seller lends the money for the purchase directly to the buyer. (See also MORTGAGE)

SETTLOR: the person who transfers his/her assets to a Family Trust for dispersion within conditions and terms laid out by him/her.

SHORT TERM RENTAL: rental of a property for a period less than a year, and typically not covered by a lease. Companies such as Airbnb engage in such rentals.

SMALL CLAIMS COURT: (in certain jurisdictions) where someone can be taken to court to recover small sums of money (varies by jurisdiction) owing to the creditor who is permitted to represent himself in court.

SNOWBIRD: people living in harsh winter areas, who typically spend the winter in warmer climes.

SOLAR PANELS: used for capturing the energy from the rays of the sun and using this power to generate electricity.

SPECIAL ASSESSMENT: this is an extra cost a condo owner pays in addition to the regular monthly maintenance fees. For example, if the parking lot needs repair and there is not enough money in the reserve fund to cover the cost, then every owner must contribute to cover that extra cost. Failure to pay may result in a lien placed on the unit.

SPECULATOR: someone engaged in the principal pursuit of buying and selling property with the sole purpose of making quick profits. (SEE FLIPPING)

STATUE OF LIMITATION: A period where legal action can only be taken to persecute certain crimes. Varies by jurisdiction.

STATUS CERTIFICATE: the Bi-laws and rules of the condominium corporation.

STRESS TEST: a financial test designed to find out how much a buyer can afford if the interest rate increases—whether they can fetch the heavier financial burden with the same income level. Some governments impose this test when the housing market accelerates, driving house prices upwards.

SURVEY: as in a Land Survey, where the boundaries of a property are laid out.

TITLE INSURANCE: a type of insurance policy that protects the homeowner from certain losses relating to transferring title; can be purchased at the time of transfer of title to the new owner.

TRUSTEE: the person or institution engaged to implement the terms and conditions of a Family Trust.

INDEX

ABOUT THE AUTHOR

JAY BRIJPAUL BSc, FRI

Jay grew up bare-footed on a farm in a remote village—Crabwood Creek in Guyana, located on the northern tip of South America, facing the Atlantic Ocean. He studied with the aid of a kerosene lamp and in 1983 graduated from the University of Guyana in Chemistry.

In January 1984, Jay landed in Winnipeg, Canada, with ten dollars in his pocket. The next day he went job hunting. "I was all dressed up in my white cotton shirt, khaki pants, a blue denim jacket, and my Guyanese plastic shoes."

Within two weeks, he found a job in a factory and in May of that year, moved to Toronto.

Jay began selling real estate in October 1988. By 1991, he was carrying three jobs—packing soap in a factory, selling real estate and life insurance. Today, he is one of Toronto's real estate veterans and one of Canada's top brokers. He was recently awarded the prestigious *Luminary of Distinction* award where new inductees have each earned over $20 million in commission during a RE/MAX career of at least 20 years.

Jay is a residential and commercial investor and conducts free workshops. "I know that if you have a strong desire to succeed and a well-planned goal, then the possibilities are endless. All you need is a good honest coach to show you the path."

In 2000, Jay founded *The Caribbean Children Foundation*, a charity that pays for surgeries for children from the Caribbean and Guyana. He continues to be involved in the real estate profession. In an attempt to pass on his vast experience and knowledge of the industry, he has written this, his first book.

ALSO FROM MIDDLEROAD PUBLISHERS

MiddleRoad | Publishers

www.middleroadpublishers.ca

ALL BOOKS AVAILABLE AT AMAZON.

eBook versions available from all eBook channels

vandalism are unsettling the citizens of Southmead.

A TIME TO LOVE AN A TIME TO DIE

By Michael Joll

Finely drawn characters. Visually dramatic, tense and emotionally satisfying, this is one of the finest novels of the Great War. In this poignant story, the writing stands in stark contrast with the unvarnished brutality of trench warfare.

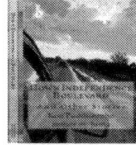

ATTITUDE

By Dave Moores

Fresh, gritty and laced with dry humour, Attitude is a fast-paced story readers of all ages won't want to put down. It's dead of winter and an outbreak of weird stuff, random acts of

DOWN INDEPENDENCE BOULEVARD AND OTHER STORIES

by Ken Puddicombe

"A brilliant collection of stories telling the tales of people forced to leave their homes…craving the past, escaping from racial conflicts and dictatorship…"—Judith Kopacsi Gelberger, author of *Heroes Don't Cry.*

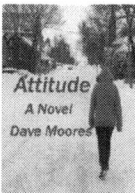

GABRIELLE

Gabrielle transcends time and space, taking the reader on a journey to Poland, France, Holland and Israel as she searches for her identity.

I WENT TO THE END OF THE RAINBOW

by Pramita Chakraborty

A beautifully illustrated, captivating tale about a young child who can't sleep and embarks on a adventure through the colours of the rainbow.

LOVE HAS TWO MOONS

By Franklin Mohan

With humour, insight and sensitivity, Franklin Mohan peels back the subtle layers of prejudice and racism in North American and Caribbean society—Raymond Holmes, author of *Witnesses and other short stories*

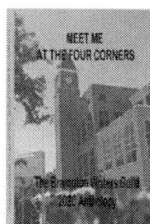

JUNTA

By Ken Puddicombe

"A gripping story (of) an imperfect democracy...the tension...builds increasingly from page to page."—Rico Downer, author of *There Once Was a Little England*

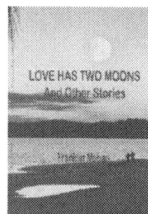

MEET ME AT THE FOUR CORNERS

Anthology

Twenty-six stories, fiction and non-Fiction, some of them prize winning submissions from the writers of the Brampton Writers' Guild, are featured in this collection.

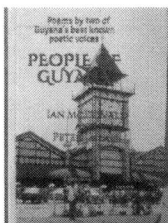

PEOPLE OF GUYANA

By Ian McDonald and
Peter Jailall

"These beautifully crafted
poems are shaped by their
generosity of spirit and
abundant capacity for empathy
and fun…" —Clem Seecharan

PERSONS OF
INTEREST

By Michael Joll

"Exotic and intriguing! Joll
brilliantly captures the reader's
interest with vivid imagery and a
relentless sleuth." —Phyllis
Humby, short story writer, poet
and novelist.

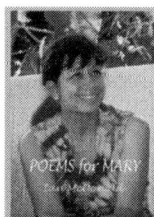

PERFECT EXECUTION
AND OTHER STORIES

by Michael Joll.

"Michael Joll is a master of
surprise endings, but they never
seem forced. He always stays
true to his characters and their
worlds." —Nancy Kay Clark,
author and editor,
CommuterLit.com

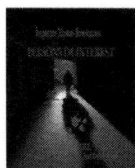

POEMS FOR MARY

By Ian Mc Donald

"The garden which my wife
has created, it is as much a work
of art as a painting by a master
spirit or a piece of perfect music
by a composer."—Ian Mc
Donald

RACING WITH THE RAIN

By Ken Puddicombe

"Puddicombe's brilliant novel...an historic political conflict in Guyana, during the Cold War and the cold cynicism and tragic irony of a state sacrificed to super-power hegemony." -Frank Birbalsingh, author of *Novels and The Nation: Essays in Canadian*

UNFATHOMABLE AND OTHER POEMS

by Ken Puddicombe

These poems cover a variety of themes, all connected to a childhood growing up in British Guiana, the rise of nationalism and the pre- and post-independence eras.

THE GARDEN

By Ian McDonald

Ian McDonald's poems are full of light and love. His easy style about the beauty of nature connects with his readers far and wide.

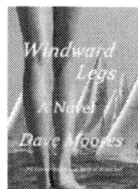

WINDWARD LEGS

By Dave Moores

A pungent cocktail of choppy romance, corporate larceny and the thrills and spills of sailboat racing, Windward Legs is the rousing and captivating story of a woman's journey to rediscover who she is.

WITNESSES AND OTHER STORIES

By Raymond Holmes

"Suspenseful, historical, futuristic and riveting...stories and characters who will stay with you." —Bruce A. Hanson, Award winning author of adult and children's fiction.

Manufactured by Amazon.ca
Bolton, ON